Youth Leadership

Josephine A. van Linden
Carl I. Fertman

Youth Leadership

A Guide to Understanding Leadership Development in Adolescents

Jossey-Bass Publishers • San Francisco

Substantial discounts on bulk quantities of Jossey-Bass books are available to corporations, professional associations, and other organizations. For details and discount information, contact the special sales department at Jossey-Bass Inc., Publishers (415) 433–1740; Fax (800) 605–2665.

For sales outside the United States, please contact your local Simon & Schuster International Office.

Jossey-Bass Web address: http://www.josseybass.com

Library of Congress Cataloging-in-Publication Data
van Linden, Josephine A.
    Youth leadership: a guide to understanding leadership development in adolescents / Josephine A. van Linden, Carl I. Fertman.—1st ed.
    p. cm.—(The Jossey-Bass education series)
    Includes bibliographical references and index.
    ISBN 0-7879-4059-3 (cloth: acid-free paper)
    1. Youth.   2. Adolescence.   3. Leadership.   I. Fertman, Carl I.
II. Title. III. Series.
    HQ796.V278   1998
    305.235—ddc21   98-9020

FIRST EDITION
HB Printing   10 9 8 7 6 5 4 3 2 1

The Jossey-Bass Education Series

Contents

List of Figures

To Josephine's dad, Harry,
who encouraged her to continually challenge herself

and to Carl's children,
Gabriel, Naomi, and Julian,
leaders today and tomorrow

Preface

We wrote *Youth Leadership* to provide insight into how leadership is developed in adolescents. During the years we have worked with adolescents, it has become apparent to us that leadership isn't a part of the average adolescent's life. Most are never offered the chance to act as leaders. Teenagers, it seems, do not come naturally to a belief in their own leadership abilities. This is not surprising, considering that adolescence is a period of intense wonderment for the teenager about who this emerging person is and how he or she fits into the larger world. However, their leadership skills are evident in everyday life, whether they realize it or not.

We didn't have to look very hard, in fact, to see that adolescents already demonstrate leadership skills and act as leaders informally every day in ways both great and small. We concluded that adolescence is an opportune time to encourage young people to explore, recognize, and celebrate their leadership potential and abilities.

What we learned both by working with youth and by doing the research required to write this book is first that *all* adolescents have leadership potential, and second that many leadership opportunities are already within reach for these young people. We learned how adolescents become leaders and how we adults can be more effective as teachers or facilitators of leadership. We also discovered strategies to help teenagers grapple with their belief in their own leadership abilities.

Writing this book has allowed us to record the knowledge we have gained throughout the years. We've connected all the dots by formulating theories based on our experience. We have found, too, that leadership development is unique to each individual; it is a creative process. The importance of this is to recognize that leadership development also furthers the emergence of healthy and risk-reducing behavior and social competence; it is an undertaking that can be an important component of *any* organization or program serving adolescents (regardless of whether the organization or program consciously espouses leadership development in serving the needs of its adolescents).

Youth Leadership is a book about how adolescents and adults can expand their views of who leaders are and what leadership is. The traditional model of leadership during adolescence holds that a few adolescents are leaders: young people who are in formal school and community organizations, holding positions as class officers and team captains. Among teens, leaders are traditionally young men and women who are popular in nonformal settings and peer groups.

Youth Leadership presents an alternative to the traditional model. It offers a three-stage model of adolescent leadership based on the real-world experience of hundreds of teenagers. Simply stated, *all* adolescents are leaders.

Who Should Read This Book?

The fundamental purpose of *Youth Leadership* is to inform and instruct those who assist youths in developing their leadership potential. The book is for adults—parents, teachers, youth workers, clergy, counselors, employers, community members, physicians, nurses, coaches, or neighbors—who want to enhance youth leadership development and opportunities.

Overview of the Contents

In Part One we introduce the concept of adolescence as a time of leadership development and review the research on who leaders are and what leadership is. We define leadership in adolescence and present a three-stage model of leadership development for adolescents (Chapter One). We focus on starting points for work in adolescent leadership (Chapter Two) and discuss the three leadership stages and their dimensions (Chapter Three).

In Chapters Four through Six (Part Two), we present the three stages of leadership development during adolescence: awareness, interaction, and mastery. In each chapter, we examine leadership development by way of a case study of one adolescent's progression through the corresponding stage of development (as well as the overall leadership development process). For each stage, we talk about how best to work with youths.

In Part Three, the focus is on nurturing and supporting adolescents so as to help them become leaders. These chapters show how adults can support youth leadership development by leading organizational change and working with educational groups (Chapter Seven); using organizations and community approaches (Chapter Eight); and facilitating leadership initiatives (Chapter Nine). Finally, in Chapter Ten we offer examples of specific efforts to expand the definition of youth leadership.

The Appendix provides additional support material in the form of results of a "leadership environment scan."

Doing Our Best as Leaders

In the summer of 1983 at the Allegheny Valley and Cornell School Districts in western Pennsylvania, our work in leadership began. Our interest focused on adolescents who were not already identified as leaders; these were kids who did not hold formal leadership positions in school activities, clubs, or sports. They were not leaders in their communities, churches, temples, or community recreation programs. We looked for young people who were not particularly popular and were not considered leaders in social and peer settings outside of school.

We began our search for teenagers by asking principals, teachers, and community youth workers to name adolescents who were leaders. We talked to these adults about why they identified these teenagers as leaders: What was it that made these kids leaders in the eyes of the adults? We then talked to the teenagers identified by the adults. We wanted to understand their perceptions of leadership. We then went back to the adults and asked them to introduce us to teenagers whom the adults thought might have leadership potential but just never seemed to show it. We talked to these young people about leadership and whether or not they were leaders. They confirmed that indeed they did not see themselves as leaders, and that leadership wasn't part of their lives. We also spoke with their parents. Unfortunately, more often than we would have hoped or imagined, the parents told us that their son or daughter was a good person, and nice, but a leader? No, not a leader. Likewise, we talked to teenagers who were not identified as leaders or having any real leadership potential. As with the previous group, neither they nor their parents identified teenagers in this third group as leaders.

It was at that point that we decided to step up and dedicate ourselves to expanding the definition of leadership and to looking for and developing the leadership potential of all adolescents, for we surely did not agree with the traditional ideas about adolescents and leadership. Since 1983, we have worked with hundreds of young people. They have joined us as part of the University of Pittsburgh Leadership Development Network on campus in the summer and in their schools and communities during the school year. This book reflects the energy that these young people as well as we and our colleagues have invested in expanding the definition of leadership among adolescents and developing the leadership potential of all teenagers.

Leaders Today and Tomorrow

Adolescents are leaders in their families, schools, and communities. They are leaders today and in the future. It is our mission to convince you, the reader, that leadership development is important not only for "your own" youth—whether they be your children, students, team members, youth group participants, employees, or neighbors—but for all those known to you and unknown. Helping youths develop their leadership potential helps us all.

March 1998

JOSEPHINE A. VAN LINDEN   CARL I. FERTMAN
Pittsburgh, Pennsylvania   *Pittsburgh, Pennsylvania*

Acknowledgments

We gratefully acknowledge those who have contributed to the development of this project and wish to offer our thanks:

- To the many adolescents who have taught us much about leadership as they developed their own ability to lead
- To our colleagues, who have worked with us throughout the years to expand the field of adolescent leadership: Yolanda Yugar, Gregg Dietz, Tom Petrone, and many others
- To the staff of the University of Pittsburgh's Maximizing Adolescent Potentials (MAPS) Program in the School of Education, who have lived and breathed leadership development
- To all of the teachers, administrators, counselors, parents, and community-based organization staff members who have learned with us about youth leadership
- To all of those listed in the references, and others, for their curiosity and ability to capture what they know—we have learned much from their experience
- To the University of Pittsburgh's School of Education, for providing a home for the Leadership Development Network and endless resources to use in our exploration of leadership development

Many funders have believed in the Leadership Development Network through the years and encouraged us to develop the best programming possible, evaluating the results so that we could constantly learn more. Without their continuing support and interest, our work would not be possible. We would like to recognize the Frick Educational Commission; Vira I. Heinz Endowment; Jewish Healthcare Foundation of Western Pennsylvania; Allegheny Conference for Community Development; Allegheny County Mental Health/Mental Retardation/Drug and Alcohol Program; Pennsylvania Departments of Education, Labor and Industry, and Health; Pittsburgh Public Schools; Catholic Diocese of Pittsburgh; Fox Chapel Area School District; Elizabeth Forward School District; Allegheny Valley School District; Cornell School District; Riverview School District; Oakland Catholic High School; Carlynton School District; Shaler Area School District; Mt. Lebanon School District; Carnegie Museums; City of Pittsburgh City Parks; Allegheny County Parks and Recreation; Allegheny Intermediate Unit; Pittsburgh New Futures; and Mon Valley Education Consortium.

We would also like to thank three special people. First, Jennifer M. Thomason gave us support, feedback, and attention to detail throughout the writing and preparation of the manuscript. Second, an anonymous reviewer suggested that we use case studies in Chapters Four, Five, and Six. Third, Daryl K. Heasley thoroughly reviewed the manuscript.

JOSEPHINE A. VAN LINDEN AND CARL I. FERTMAN

The Authors

Josephine A. van Linden is an adjunct faculty member for the Professional Leadership Master's Program and the director of the Leadership Development Network, now located at Carlow College in Pittsburgh.

As an adolescent, Josephine spent every Friday night and Saturday and Sunday afternoons making chocolate sundaes at the soda fountain in Corbetts Pharmacy. After she graduated from Munhall High School, she attended Villa Maria College in Erie, Pennsylvania. She graduated with a bachelor of science degree in home economics education and holds a master's degree in public health.

Van Linden was a teacher for more than twelve years at Steel Valley High School, where she learned to love young people, particularly in the stage of their lives called adolescence. She moved on from teaching the traditional cooking and sewing classes when she became department chair; she began to devote her time instead to teaching life skills, family relations, and child development. She also coordinated a school-parent group dealing with adolescent use of drugs and alcohol.

As director of the Leadership Development Network, she continues to work with both adolescents and adults to develop leadership in all adolescents.

Carl I. Fertman is associate professor and executive director of the Maximizing Adolescent Potentials (MAPS) Program in the School of Education at the University of Pittsburgh. He is the founder and director of the Pennsylvania Service Learning Evaluation Network, also located at the University of Pittsburgh.

As a teenager, Fertman worked after school, on weekends, and during the summer at his family's small business, Cornell Uniform, as a truck driver. When he wasn't working he attended Abington High School, where he was a member of the debate and tennis teams. He went on to get an undergraduate degree from Philadelphia College of Textiles and Science and a master's of business administration from Temple University in Philadelphia.

He served in Colombia and Chile as a Peace Corps volunteer, where he designed, implemented, and evaluated vocational education and training programs for mentally and physically challenged adolescents. On returning to the United States, he worked as a counselor and director in a number of community agencies in Philadelphia and Pittsburgh. He came to the University of Pittsburgh in the early 1980s to earn a Ph.D. in rehabilitation counseling.

Since 1982, Fertman has done research, taught, and worked to promote the mental health of adolescents. He works extensively with schools and community agencies throughout Pennsylvania to support and nurture adolescents.

Youth Leadership

Part One

The Potential for Adolescent Leadership

Adolescence is a busy time; adolescents spend it sorting out their lives and their futures. They experience a transition during which they give up the freedoms of childhood, learn the new roles they will take on as adults, experience uncertainties about their future, and wonder and worry about whether they will fail or succeed when it is their time to contribute to society. They try to answer the questions "Who am I?" and "Where do I fit in?" (Ianni, 1989, pp. 22–23).

One part of making the transition from child to adult is learning about leadership. *Who are leaders? What is leadership? Could I be a leader?* Unfortunately, most adolescents answer this last question, "No, I am not a leader."

In Chapter One, we discuss how adolescents themselves think about leadership. We define leadership from both a transactional and transformational point of view so that we can study leadership development from angles that are often missed. After reading this chapter, you will have a better idea of how teenagers can develop their leadership abilities and potentials.

Chapter Two illustrates how theories about adolescent development relate to understanding the emergence of leadership in adolescents. Examining the similarities and differences between adolescents also gives a clearer picture of the process.

Our approach, outlined in Chapter Three, divides leadership development into stages. These stages are further broken down into dimensions, which provide a basis for a better understanding of leadership development in adolescence.

Chapter One

Seeing Adolescents as Leaders

You kiddin' me? I'm into a lot of things—girls,
parties, sex, bein' with my friends, ya know? Sure,
my mom's buggin' me I gotta do this 'n' that—do
better in this, pay attention at school, and that.
But my dad's the worst, of course. What do I think
about? What CDs I wanna buy, tapes I wanna get,
places I wanna hang out at. Yeah, sometimes I
think about school. Ya know, that's scary. School
is tough for me; I have to work hard. Some of
them teachers just seem to have it in for me, I don't
know. Bein' a leader? I don't think about bein' a
leader or who the leaders are. It's not part of my life.

—*Luis, tenth grade*

I'm in student council. I'm going to college. I'm
gonna do a lot of stuff. I guess I'm a leader in
school. I'll be a leader in college, too.

—*Tanisha, twelfth grade*

Bein' on the street, it's hard to think. I thinkin'
'bout who's takin' care of me, who's watchin' me.
I gotta watch out for them, watchin' out for each
other. That's what we're tryin' to do. Tryin' to stay
together, to protect our property, our neighborhood,
our women, our girls, our babies. That's what we
tryin' to do. Bein' a leader in that situation, with

things goin' down and that, I don't know. Sure, I a
leader. Teacher don't think so, police don't think
so. My people know I a leader. I in charge. They
listen to me.

—*Ray, ninth grade*

I remember when she was in school, I never thought
of her bein' a leader. She had a baby when she was
seventeen. Didn't make no sense to me. Went out
and did her own stuff and now to see her in the
community, bein' active, I can't figure it out. I can't
figure out how it happened, why it happened. But
there she is, real comfortable gettin' up at meetin's
and talkin' 'bout what's goin' on. I respect her, ya
know? I respect her a lot.

—*Marie, mother and grandmother,*
talking about her daughter, now age twenty

When I think back about kids I've seen, kids I know,
what they've done, it's really hard for me to think
about them. I look more at where they ended up in
life. I don't think about them being leaders; yes,
some have gone on to become presidents of boards,
successful in business. A lot have gotten married;
many haven't. Yet, you know, most of them—
they just live quiet lives in the neighborhood.
I'm not quite sure they're not better leaders
than the others, in their own ways, in their own
communities.

—*H. Dorsett, teacher*

I guess maybe I'm a leader. I don't know.
Leadership is somethin', maybe I could have. It's
not like a disease. I'm not sure exactly how it is out
there. Sounds like something that could be inside

me. I just wonder if maybe I'm not focused on it.
It's not important to me. It's not a part of my life.
Maybe it's there and maybe sometime I'll know
this side of me. But right now, I'm having fun.
There'll be time later for being a leader. Right now,
I'm having fun.

—Laura, eleventh grade

Few adolescents think about leadership. They have other priorities in life. This doesn't mean they're not interested in or concerned about their leadership abilities and potential. It simply reflects reality for most adolescents. The words of Luis, Tanisha, Ray, Marie, H. Dorsett, and Laura present typical views of teenagers and adults toward adolescent leadership.

Luis, a tenth grader, puts it well when he says: "I don't know. Bein' a leader? I don't think about bein' a leader or who the leaders are. It's not part of my life." Even so, today's teenagers are tomorrow's leaders. Sometimes it is difficult to picture teenagers as future leaders, while at other times their destinies seem clear. You can hear it in the words of Tanisha: "I'll be a leader in college." The truth is that as much as we might like to be able to predict their life trajectories, we cannot tell what the future may bring for specific individuals within a group of adolescents; we cannot predict who will have the strongest leadership abilities. It may be comforting to believe we can, but this is false hope; in the end it detracts from the opportunity to work with *all* adolescents to develop their potential both as human beings and leaders.

Researchers tell us that leadership development starts early. Gardner (1987) concluded that the skills critical for effective leadership, including the capacity to understand and interact with others, develop strikingly in adolescence and especially in young adulthood. But they begin to form before five years of age. Research has found few differences between those adolescents identified as student leaders and those not identified as such. No major differences were found using either quantitative or qualitative research methods. The researchers concluded that it is not possible to predict exceptional leadership performance in adolescents (Garrod, 1988). This supports our assertion that all teenagers have the potential to lead.

Clearly, adolescents do have the potential to become leaders in the workplace, in their families, in the community, and in government. Many schools, community agencies, religious institutions, youth organizations, and sports programs have incorporated leadership development in young people as part of their missions. Certainly, part of growing up is learning about leadership through people and activities. Some adolescents may even participate in formal leadership training through school activities, scout groups, 4-H clubs, boys and girls clubs, or religious organizations. Observing how others lead and how they fit into this process happens naturally with young people; however, learning about leadership doesn't necessarily mean that an adolescent will feel like a leader, know that he or she has leadership skills, or even have any desire to be a leader.

Adolescents are busy leading in many ways—maybe not as presidents of their class or members of student government, but in more subtle ways. They are baby-sitting, working a job, and volunteering. They are spending time with peers, hanging out at the mall, and being involved in school or community—activities that all help adolescents develop their own personal understanding of leadership. Leadership is not something that is reserved for a few accomplished students. All teenagers can learn about leadership and define for themselves what it means. Students who might have behavior problems in the community and in school develop their own ideas about leadership, as Ray's own words boldly demonstrate: "Sure, I a leader. Teacher don't think so, police don't think so. But my people know I a leader. I in charge. They listen to me." Clearly, leadership development begins at an early age and continues throughout every person's life.

Many adults are not quite sure how leadership develops in adolescents. Marie, a mother and grandmother, conveys a sense of the mystery many adults accept in explaining their children's leadership development: "I can't figure out how it happened, why it happened. But there she is, real comfortable gettin' up at meetin's and talkin' 'bout what's goin' on. I respect her, ya know? I respect her a lot."

Even if adults don't quite understand how to help adolescents become aware of their leadership skills, the skills are valued. Even if adults find the concept of leadership unclear, they want adolescents to demonstrate leadership abilities. Many parents hope that their children will take traditional leadership roles in formal school and community activities and organizations. Still, sometimes the adults' confusion about the issue is unintentionally interpreted by the adolescents as meaning, "You cannot be a leader."

Employers are more interested in adolescents who are leaders. For many employers, this initially equates with being at work on time, doing the job, and not causing problems. Over time, though, employers assess youths' leadership in the workplace in the form of taking on more responsibility and showing concern about the quality of the work being done. Leadership in the workplace is also often confused with the concepts of management and supervision. These can be particularly overwhelming notions for adolescents, and their fear of "bossing" can keep them from exploring their leadership potential.

Leadership is an elusive concept. This is in part because adults and adolescents alike do not define themselves in terms of leadership. If you talk to adults about where they use their leadership skills, they respond by citing job titles: teacher, lawyer, mechanic, nurse, writer, salesperson, or carpenter. Ask for more detail about their professions, and the responses are likely to reflect technical aspects of their work with a specific group of people, products, or equipment. Adults generally do not perceive themselves as exercising their leadership skills in all parts of their daily lives. Similarly, adolescents might concede that they changed a friend's point of view on a certain subject, or that their friends listen to them. But when asked if he or she leads discussions or influences decisions, an adolescent is apt to answer, "Well, not really."

What Is Leadership?

Researchers who are interested in defining leadership continue to come up with new information. One safe generalization, based on studies conducted in the past forty years, is that leadership is not nearly as mysterious as has commonly been thought. Peters and Austin (1985) believed that leadership connotes unleashing energy, building, freeing, and growing. Halloran and Benton (1987) defined leadership as the ability to influence the actions of others; a person who is seen to influence others' actions in either formal or informal settings is labeled a leader. The ability to motivate others to follow a common cause is another way to identify leadership. These are not the only ways, however. According to Bennis and Nanus (1985), all people have leadership potential. They lead in many places, and in many ways, every day. An individual's ability to use his or her skills and to recognize the situational influences that can support and promote leadership is critical to the realization of leadership potential.

If everyone (even young people) has leadership potential, then why is there a struggle for adults and adolescents to recognize, develop, and celebrate their leadership potential? The answer is that leadership is complex; it is not a simple concept. Understanding and appreciating the complexity of leadership is a prerequisite to supporting and challenging teenagers to be the best leaders they can be.

Transformational and Transactional Leadership

When researchers first began to study leadership, much of their attention focused on the traits and situations that can affect leadership development. Over time, the concept of leadership evolved into something more dynamic. It was thought to be contingent on a transaction or exchange between the leader and the led (Holander, 1986). This model is known as *transactional leadership*. In this view, leaders exchange promises of rewards and benefits to subordinates for the subordinates' fulfillment of agreements with the leader. This type of leadership is product-oriented: the leader sets up the rules and procedures to make a product, and those led comply with the rules and follow the procedures to produce the product. To be a leader under this model means to "do." This type of leader is in charge at meetings, makes decisions, tells people what to do, speaks to groups, and writes letters and memos.

This definition of leadership is not wholly satisfactory; leadership involves much more than mere transaction between people. Leaders embody ideals with which other people identify. Leadership involves helping people transcend their own self-interests for the good of the group, organization, or society; consider their long-term needs to develop themselves, rather than their immediate needs; and generally become more aware of what is really important. Downton (1973) and Burns (1978) developed this more inclusive model and called it *transformational leadership*. Its focus is on the process of "being" a leader, helping people transform themselves from followers into leaders.

Originally, people were thought to be either transactional or transformational leaders. Over time, however, the theory has evolved and now reflects the fact that people can be both. Transactional leadership focuses on the skills and tasks associated with leadership, such as public speaking, writing, delegating authority, leading meetings, and making decisions. This is what people who are leaders do. Transformational leadership focuses on the process of leadership and what it means to be a leader. It is concerned with how individuals use their abilities to influence people. We think of the difference between transactional and transformational leadership as doing leadership tasks versus being a leader. They are both important aspects of leadership.

Researchers (Lyons, Saltonstall, and Hanmer, 1990) support this view in their study on how adolescent girls view leadership. Two modes of leadership were found among a group of students that included both girls identified as student leaders in their schools and ones who were not. The first mode of leadership is called being an "interdependent leader" in relation to others; it is contrasted with the mode favored by the "autonomous leader":

> The interdependent leader will make sure everyone's ideas are included in a larger plan of action, which the leader has synthesized and then brought to her group. In this process an actual decision may be the last step in a series of smaller "decisions" already achieved by the act of listening to everyone's ideas. In contrast, for "autonomous" leaders the burden lies in an accurate identification of a problem and in offering a unique and fitting solution. The decision itself is a kind of test of both the leader's analysis of the problem and the prescription for its solution. In the moment of decision making for the autonomous leader, the emphasis will be on persuading one's constituents that both are right. [Lyons, Saltonstall, and Hanmer, 1990, pp. 195–196]

In addition, the researchers note that "In evaluating the two leadership modes, it is clear there are strengths and weakness[es] of each. For effective leadership, a balance and flexibility in both modes may be necessary, especially considering the context of leadership" (p. 207).

Leadership Environment

Leadership and leaders involve social processes. Leaders are evident among all people, regardless of their culture, whether they are isolated Indian villagers, nomads of the Eurasian steppes, or Polynesian fisher-folk (Smith and Krueger, 1933). No society is known that does not have leadership in some aspect of its social life, although many lack a solitary leader who makes and enforces decisions (Bass, 1990). Each society has its own beliefs, traditions, rites of passage, myths, and celebrations of leaders and leadership.

Not only is leadership reflective of the larger society or environment but it is also shaped and molded within specific organizations, groups, and situations. Hersey and Blanchard (1982) recognized that leadership looks different in various situations. According to them, leadership is flexible and adaptable. It differs between a situation that involves completing a task with people who are unknown to an individual (such that the individual—the leader—delegates authority and tells people what to do) and one in which a similar task is accomplished between friends. In the latter case, an individual's energetic and enthusiastic participation as an equal might be considered leadership.

Developmental Process

A person does not wake up one day as a leader. Leadership is a personal and developmental process. This development takes place over time, throughout a person's life. In fact, differences in individual development form the basis of a theory of transformational leadership by Kuhnert and Lewis (1987), who suggest that such leadership reflects the mature adult development of personal standards and transcendental values. In contrast, those who pursue only transactional approaches to leadership are arrested at lower levels of development that are built around their own immediate needs, feelings, and interpersonal connections.

Tasks of Adolescence

Our experience has been that any initiative to develop adolescent leadership potential must be planned in light of basic facts about adolescent development. Adolescence is a time of change and transition, usually encompassing the ages of ten to nineteen, the second decade of a person's life. Individuals during this time exhibit tremendous diversity in their physical development, maturity levels, behavior, and understanding of the world and of themselves. Because adolescents' needs, characteristics, and tasks alter drastically during this ten-year period, it is often broken into two parts: early (ten to fourteen) and late adolescence (fifteen to nineteen). Figures 1.1 and 1.2 highlight specific needs of early and late adolescence. These needs reflect the *primary tasks of adolescence*, through which individuals develop a sense of who they are and how they view their world. Adolescents' idealism, quest for independence, and identity formation are critical to this process and to leadership development.

Idealism

Adolescents are idealists. Idealism comes from their emerging ability to think about their expanded world. With abstract reasoning, they also develop the capability to envision possible solutions to social problems (untempered by actual experience). They conceive notions

Figure 1.1 Some Specific Needs of the Early Adolescent (Ten to Fourteen Years Old)

1. Understanding of physical and emotional changes that take place during puberty. These are very personal and frequently troublesome matters. The child needs help in understanding himself during this period of change and in understanding the idea that it is healthy to grow and evolve.

2. Self-acceptance. The adolescent is beginning to resolve the conflict between what she is and what she wishes to be. She is beginning to establish life goals and make reasonable plans to attain those goals.

3. Acceptance of and by others. The adolescent is developing acceptable relationships with peers of both sexes, making friends, getting to know others, and understanding their differences. This includes realization of the effect he has on others as opposed to the effect he wants to have. He begins to understand the dynamics of peer pressure.

4. Acceptance, understanding, approval, and love from significant adults.

5. Knowledge of responsibility to others. The adolescent is learning not to be completely self-centered and is learning self-control.

6. Discovering how to make decisions, assume responsibility, use independent judgment, and recognize and accept the consequences of actions.

7. Figuring out how to deal with feelings. Adolescents become aware that others experience feelings similar to their own.

8. The beginnings of a personal value system.

of ideal families, ideal schools, ideal religious institutions, and ideal societies; they may rebel against the imperfect ones they see around them. The young adolescent cannot understand why the rest of the world does not accept her idealistic solutions to social, economic, and sociological problems (Muuss, 1980). They may become angry and express unwillingness to accept reality; or, as is frequently the case, they may ally themselves with underdogs or those they see as less fortunate than themselves. Although this behavior is sometimes frustrating to adults who must combat adolescent passion, one researcher points out that "active imagination and the dreaming of ideals are not wasteful activities . . . but can be a constructive part of everyone's life, making for the improvement of human functioning in a socially meaningful way" (Menge, 1982, p. 419).

This idealism continues through late adolescence, often taking the form of social activism. Many adolescents become involved in social, political, or religious causes, giving them an opportunity to explore their ideals and gain experience in the real world.

Idealism begins to diminish near the end of late adolescence. This is a result of increased cognitive capabilities and exposure to

Figure 1.2 Some Specific Needs of the Late Adolescent (Fifteen to Nineteen Years Old)

1. *Sexuality:* The adolescent needs to understand that sexual feelings are normal, needs to know about her reproductive capabilities, has to learn how sexual expression relates to her other feelings, and has to understand the emotional issues surrounding sexual intimacy.

2. *Status:* The adolescent needs opportunities to gain a sense of competence in sports, academics, and social activities. He also must make more of his own decisions and then accept responsibility for those choices.

3. *Sociality:* Adolescents need opportunities to try out different roles as they continue to form their identities.

4. *Values and Morality:* As he or she forms the frame of reference through which to view the world, the adolescent needs to discuss opinions, experiences, thoughts, and feelings in an atmosphere of caring trust and acceptance with both peers and adults.

the ideas and beliefs of others. Late adolescents move beyond abstract reasoning to the formulation of a set of values, an ethical system that guides their behavior. They also begin to view other perspectives as separate from their own. As they gain more experience at work or in college, their frame of reference is modified by exposure to the conflicting or confirming views of others (Cobb, 1992).

Quest for Independence

The quest for independence and autonomy plays a powerful role during early adolescence. The emergence of self-understanding and self-reflection allows young people to begin to differentiate themselves from their parents and teachers, and instead compare themselves with their peers. Juhasz (1982) noted that during this stage, adolescents begin to seek identities separate from their parents and try to somehow make a difference in a wider social perspective. At the same time, they remain quite aware of their dependence. This duality often creates both internal and external conflict. Adolescents expend considerable energy moving toward greater control over their lives and increased freedom from authority, while at the same time trying to hold on to the benefits and security of childhood (Thornburg, 1983).

As adolescents grow older, they make more decisions for themselves, and the number of decisions they make with parents and teachers decreases. The types of decisions being made and the people responsible for those decisions are the central issues of independence in late adolescence. Who to spend time with; what classes to take; and when to study, do chores, and work are examples of daily decisions adolescents make. Although these decisions appear to be trivial, they are essential in the adolescent's process of separating from his parents so that he can become his own person. Living with the consequences of previous decisions helps adolescents successfully resolve later decisions. As older adolescents become increasingly confident in their ability to make decisions, they begin to feel that they are in charge of their lives (Cobb, 1992).

Identity Formation

Early adolescence is a critical period for identity formation. Who they are and how they fit into the world are defining issues for ten-to-fourteen-year-olds. It is during this stage of development that individuals begin to establish and clarify a social conscience and work toward learning socially responsible behavior (Havighurst, 1972; Kohlberg and Hersh, 1977). Erikson (1980) indicated that during the early stages of this period (from ten to twelve years of age), individuals define themselves by what they can do and by the skills they possess. As individuals progress through this stage (from twelve to fifteen), they begin to clarify their role in their world (in school and the local community) and define and refine their individuality. They look for role models and heroes and try to integrate aspects of those ideals into their own value systems (George and Alexander, 1993).

The social hierarchy of the school and community becomes immensely important during this stage of a person's life. Teachers continue to play an important role in affirming a sense of competence and role expectations for individuals.

Identity formation continues in late adolescence and does not fully emerge until early adulthood, although most of the process is completed during adolescence. By their midteens (fifteen to seventeen), adolescents' sense of self includes who they have been, as well as who they hope to become. They define themselves more in terms of their intentions—what they would like to do—than by what they have actually done. As their ability to think abstractly develops, older adolescents can reflect on past behaviors and plan for the future (Cobb, 1992).

Identity formation is the culmination of many aspects of the self. Erikson (1968) views the formation of identity as making decisions about occupational, political, religious, and gender roles.

Marcia (1980, 1988) writes of identity as an organization of beliefs, attitudes, habits, and motives into a continuing personal history. He believes that adolescents who manage to establish their identity explore more options, whether they be personal or vocational opportunities. These adolescents tend to be more tolerant of individual differences, allowing the same freedom of self-definition in others as they do in themselves.

Adolescents and Leadership

Discussion of the tasks of adolescence provides a guide for understanding leadership development within the framework of adolescence. It highlights the developmental struggles that teenagers face as they answer the questions "Who am I?" and "How do I fit in?" To be meaningful to adolescents, leadership development must consider their idealism, quest for independence, and identity formation. Leadership development within the framework of adolescents' needs can be a creative and useful vehicle for involving teens and helping them to make a difference. It focuses on providing possible solutions for the issues and problems that adolescents find important. Leadership development gives adolescents a voice in the decision-making processes that affect their lives.

For us, the framework of adolescence calls attention to the need for young people to answer questions about their own leadership abilities. Through life experience, observation of the people around them, and maybe even education, teenagers arrive at adolescence with a model for doing leadership tasks: leading meetings, speaking in public, and acting as class presidents or team captains. Clearly, in the eyes of an adolescent one either does leadership tasks or doesn't. Unfortunately, this fact leads many teenagers and adults to incorrectly assume that most teenagers think leadership just isn't a cool thing to do, and that teenagers aren't and can't be leaders. This is not the case. The problem is that most adults and adolescents rely on a definition of leadership that focuses on the transactional model of "doing leadership tasks." This limited view is out of sync with the lives of teenagers; it does not take into account the developmental struggles they face.

We argue that all people, including adolescents, have leadership potential. This doesn't mean that every adolescent will be recognized for his or her leadership skills—or even know that those abilities exist. It also doesn't mean we can predict how and where a person's leadership potential will manifest itself. H. Dorsett, the high school teacher quoted at the beginning of this chapter, summarized this notion in discussing his past students. Like any other skill—whether athletic, artistic, mechanical, or intellectual—leadership is shared by everyone to some extent. For example, most adolescents clearly have a capacity for music. Even though few adolescents are famous composers, opera singers, or musicians, every teenager at least enjoys listening to music, dancing, or singing out loud to a favorite song. In much the same way, every adolescent has the capacity to lead.

It makes sense that teenagers may be reluctant to lead; it is an effort, both mentally and socially, and leadership may not seem to have much to do with real-life experience. Whether they are simply unaware of their potential, unsure of how to start the process, or already interested in doing more to develop their leadership skills, adolescents need help to tap their leadership abilities. Encouraging them to do so benefits everyone, both now and in the future.

For our purpose, we define leaders as individuals (both adults and adolescents) who think for themselves, communicate their thoughts and feelings to others, and help others understand and act on their own beliefs; they influence others in an ethical and socially responsible way. For many, leadership is best described as a physical sensation: a need to share ideas, energy, and creativity, and not let personal insecurities be an obstacle. Being a leader means trusting one's instincts, both when doing leadership tasks and being a leader.

Defining leadership in this way allows both adolescents and adults to look at leadership in a new light. The basic premise of this definition is that leadership is a set of skills and attitudes that can be learned and practiced, and that all adolescents can develop these skills and attitudes. The definition is broad enough to include students who are not currently seen as leaders in their schools, communities, or homes, as well as those who already demonstrate their leadership skills and attitudes in more obvious ways. It encourages all teenagers to explore their individual potential as leaders, and it calls out to schools, families, and communities to create an environment that fosters leadership, allowing youth to realize and practice their leadership skills in a safe environment.

In this book we present a model of leadership for adolescents that includes both transactional and transformational leadership—doing leadership tasks and being a leader. Including both is the most effective way to support and guide adolescent leadership development. Transactional leadership focuses on the skills of leadership, while transformational leadership is being the leader one already is. Adolescence is a time of opportunity in which to awaken the leadership potential of individuals; it is a time to help adolescents be the leaders they already are. We consider leadership to be flexible and adaptable. It is reflective of the people, situations, and tasks involved, and its realization requires a creative process of self-discovery and hard work.

To fully develop leadership potential and abilities, adolescents must pass through a series of stages, acquiring knowledge of transactional and transformational leadership and of their corresponding information, attitudes, and skills. It is critical that the leadership development model include a balance of transactional and transformational leadership. Here are their characteristics:

Transformational Leadership

Values the participation and contribution of others

Takes all viewpoints and advice into account before making a decision

Considers individuals within their contexts and situations

Uses individuals to test decisions

Develops the self first to be a better contributor to the group

Learns from experiences to generalize to "real life"

Recognizes the importance of the process

Shares leadership (group power)

Transactional Leadership

Values problem and solution identification

Makes decisions—even if everyone has not been heard—
in order to move forward

Uses standards and principles as guides in decision making

Develops the self to be a better decision maker for the group

Gets things done

Recognizes the importance of the product

Takes charge (personal power)

Stages of Leadership Development

The stages of adolescent leadership development are sequential but fluid. Individuals may move from one stage to the next, only to return to the previous stage when they encounter a new situation. Stage One focuses on initial *awareness* of one's leadership potential and abilities. Adolescents in Stage One need help to see themselves as leaders. In Stage Two, they expand and strengthen their leadership potential and abilities; in this stage we see growth in leadership skills and confidence solidified through *interaction*. Mastery of leadership skills in specific areas and activities of life is the focus of Stage Three. In each leadership development stage, young people acquire leadership information and attitudes, and an array of interpersonal skills (communication, decision making, and stress management).

When working with adolescents, we want to appreciate their diversity, creativity, and energy. More important, we want to help them see themselves as having a capacity to lead. We need to make the concept of leadership concrete, so they can grasp it, get their hands around it, and mold it to their lives. In adolescence, leadership is manifested in more ways than standing up in front of a group to speak, planning a dance, or leading a meeting. It's an energy, an ability, that reveals itself in a variety of ways. It should be celebrated and encouraged.

Leadership Concerns of Adolescents

For themselves and others, young people's views about leadership impede believing in adolescent leadership. As we learned from Luis, Tanisha, Ray, and Laura, most adolescents do not even think about leadership. When they do, they usually don't think of it in relation to themselves. In the majority of cases, they view leadership as something formal and distant. It is only for the popular kids, for those who make things happen; it is something adults have and teens don't; it is being the boss, doing the right thing. It is, young people and many adults insist, difficult to attain.

Adults and adolescents alike tend to define the concept of leadership in limited ways. There is a certain set of characteristics that they associate with leadership (Figure 1.3). It is possible for such characteristics to play a role in leadership, but they are not the sole determinants of leadership ability. Even if they do possess a few of these characteristics, adolescents often believe that they have no chance of being leaders because it is risky to stand apart from their peers and show their individuality.

These characteristics make for a narrow definition of leadership. Knowing this, we find it easy to predict how adolescents respond if you ask them who the leaders are in their schools. They point out class officers, student council members, and talented athletes: a small group of students elected or otherwise chosen whenever a leadership opportunity arises. However, this definition limits the kinds of people who fit the "leadership profile." Most students do not see themselves as part of such a group; therefore, most high school students don't think of themselves as having leadership

Figure 1.3 Characteristics Adolescents
Associate with Being a Leader

Tall	Older	Having sense of duty
Physically fit	Honest	Healthy
Self-confident	Not overweight	Male
Reliable	Popular	Physically energetic
Attractive	Intelligent	Desiring to excel
Possessing initiative	Well behaved	Maintaining good
Wealthy	in school	attendance
Persistent	Hardworking	Having good
Extroverted	Willful	school habits
	(having willpower)	

potential. For example, the adolescent who is basically quiet in new situations has a difficult time thinking that she could be a leader. It is almost impossible for most adolescents to live up to their own demanding image of leadership.

A further complication in adolescents' understanding of leadership is that they often adhere to traditional ideas about how a person *becomes* a leader. Many believe what is commonly known as the "great person" theory of leadership: leaders are born, not made. The premise in this line of thinking is that inheritance and destiny make a limited number of people qualified for leadership; only those with the right upbringing, such as John F. Kennedy and Eleanor Roosevelt, can lead. Another common notion is that great events make leaders out of otherwise-ordinary people. According to this theory, Martin Luther King, Jr., was simply there when the civil rights movement began, and it propelled him into a position of leadership. Although such theories as these are inadequate in describing what makes a leader, they permeate the thinking of many adolescents.

Adolescents' motivation for being leaders is underdeveloped. They are often concerned about the responsibilities of leadership and are afraid they won't be able to make the right decisions if placed in a position of authority. Furthermore, adolescents tell us that they are unsure that leadership is either attainable or desirable. If adolescents believe they are not leaders, they aren't likely to seek opportunities to develop their leadership potential; thus their belief becomes a self-fulfilling prophecy.

Even after accepting the idea that they too can be leaders, it is difficult for adolescents (and adults, for that matter) to understand that the path to leadership is rich with opportunities to demonstrate leadership ability. These opportunities can fall into an adolescent's lap, or they can be formed using a little ingenuity and creativity. One illustration of the latter path is Tara, an average student at a large city high school.

Intrigued by the issue of AIDS, Tara chose this to be the subject of her term paper for English. She decided that instead of doing the research for her paper in the library, she would go out and talk to people who were actually living with AIDS. None of her friends were conducting this sort of research, but she felt driven nonetheless to take that extra step. In the phone book, she located community-based organizations that provide services to AIDS patients, and through this connection she set up interviews with three individuals. She audiotaped her sessions and then wrote her paper from the material she had on tape, using the library only for background information on the virus. When Tara turned in her project, she felt good about how much she had learned. She was enlightened not only by the negative side—the hopelessness—of the disease but also by the humor and strength of the people she interviewed. Her teacher was so impressed by the project that he submitted it to a citywide English writing competition. Tara won. She had never won anything before and hadn't even come close to doing so academically. Tara is a leader. She didn't become president of student council or captain of a sports team at school. Instead, what she gained was the confidence and trust of others, who came to value and respect her ideas. In addition, Tara's interest in writing was sparked, and she went on to study journalism.

Negative Leadership

One force that can block adolescent leadership development is what we refer to as negative leadership. Some teenagers do in fact demonstrate strong leadership abilities: they motivate their peers, they voice their opinions, and their behavior matches their words. But when they put their skills to use, the outcome is negative. Their leadership results in delinquent behavior in the form of dropping out of school, involvement with violence, and teen pregnancy, among other problems. Gang leaders, drug pushers, and juvenile criminals are examples of negative leaders. Based on their experiences, these teens have learned they can be noticed, exert power, and make a difference in their own lives and the lives of others. In their world, this negative behavior provokes the same esteem and regard that positive leadership inspires in the dominant culture.

Negative leadership is rooted in repression, poverty of the soul, and violence. Many might characterize it as behavior born out of the instinct to survive in a hostile environment: a family, community, school, or group of peers that is hurtful to an adolescent. We don't condone this behavior, but it is damaging to label it as antisocial and destructive without looking at the behavior within the context of its larger psychosocial framework. For example, teenagers who served with the Guardian Angels in the 1980s were viewed by many as youths who demonstrated leadership in addressing social issues in large urban areas of the United States. Others viewed them as vigilantes, delinquents, and bums who inappropriately took the law into their own hands.

In the 1990s, the issue of negative leadership has become a major concern. This is due primarily to the increase in violent crimes among youth—in particular, the negative impact of guns. Geoffrey Canada says in *Fist, Stick, Knife, Gun,* "Even more dangerous than the fact that there are tens of thousands of adolescents shooting and playing with guns is the psychological impact that having a gun has on these kids. There were always natural checks and balances on violence among young people before handguns were so common. . . . Kids with guns see no limits on their power" (1995, p. 100). The dominant culture sees these adolescents not as leaders, but rather as criminals. However, within their cultures, some adolescents perceive their peers with guns as leaders. Indeed, the latter often show many strong leadership characteristics.

The concept of negative leadership is important because it calls attention to the need to understand the cultural context of behavior. This doesn't mean we should condone the behavior, but rather understand why the behavior is displayed. Furthermore, understanding the cultural context shows us that interventions to change negative leadership behavior require an "ecological" approach, one that considers the family and community as well as the individual.

Adults who work with adolescents to develop leadership must help them clear the obstacles to their seeing themselves as leaders. Adults need to accept the challenge involved in helping adolescents recognize the many opportunities to lead that lie within their reach. Adults must see the negative leadership that destroys youth and community alike, and redirect the energy of negative leaders by working with families within the community.

Adolescent leadership is shown in a young person who speaks out on important community issues and in one who simply shovels snow from an elderly neighbor's walk without being asked. Leadership is demonstrated every day in myriad ways by adolescents in their families, schools, workplaces, and communities. Leadership development may be so subtle that the youths themselves never realize they have leadership skills at all, and therefore view leadership as distant and unattainable. For others, the process is active and self-fulfilling. Clearly, we want to call attention to this process. In our work to expand leadership development, we raise awareness in adults and adolescents alike that leadership potential and ability exists in all adolescents.

Chapter Two

Adolescent Developmental Needs

Young people bring many strengths and useful
experiences to the tasks of adolescence: seemingly
limitless energy, great curiosity about the world, an
intense desire to learn skills, and a trusting attitude.

—A Matter of Time (1992, p. 9)

I think everyone has it. They're not thinking about it,
and they're not talking about it, but it's there.

—Alexia, twelfth grade

People wait for someone to make them a leader. You know,
promoting them to a crew chief, supervisor, manager, or
captain. A job title doesn't make someone a leader.

—Steve, eleventh grade

Taking turns is leadership; so is sharing, taking responsibility, caring, or following. Being a good follower,
participating, understanding what is going on, they
are all part of learning about the leader inside.

—Pedro, twelfth grade

We see leadership development as a dynamic process. Our hope is
for young people to arrive at adolescence with an awareness of their
leadership knowledge, attitudes, and skills. There is, of course, still
the question of whether it is even possible for young people to
understand their leadership potential while still in adolescence, for

we have found that leadership development among adolescents is not recognized. Yet we know that all teenagers can develop their leadership potential through experiences with people, activities, and learning across four settings: their family, community, school, and workplace. We have also found that when teenagers are helped to develop their leadership abilities, they become more aware of their leadership potential as well.

We want to overcome the shortcomings of the current approach to leadership development during the teenage years, which focuses on a select group of youths and is primarily limited to transactional leadership development (as we discussed in Chapter One). The chapter reviews the work of four theoreticians on the subject of adolescent development. It then discusses the ways in which adolescents differ from one another, while concluding with a summary of what we believe is more important than individual differences: the commonalities shared among most teenagers.

Theories of Adolescent Development

To deepen our understanding of adolescents, and thereby make our job a little easier, we begin with a survey of the work of four theoreticians of adolescent development.

All You Need Is Love

Abraham Maslow's theories (1970) have helped to change our perceptions so that we can see adolescents as whole people. Maslow suggests that humans have a *hierarchy of needs,* which ranges from lower-level needs for survival and safety to higher-level needs for intellectual achievement and self-actualization. *Self-actualization* is Maslow's term for self fulfillment, the realization of personal potential. Figure 2.1 is a diagram of Maslow's model.

Maslow (1968) calls the four lower-level needs (survival, safety, self-esteem, and belonging) *deficiency needs.* When these needs are satisfied, the motivation for fulfilling them decreases. He labels the

Figure 2.1 Maslow's Hierarchy of Needs

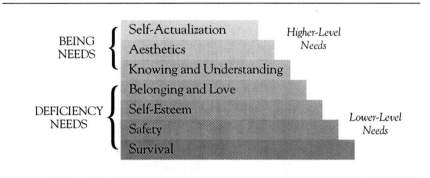

Source: Adapted from Maslow, 1970.

three higher-level needs (intellectual achievement, aesthetic appreciation, and self-actualization) *being needs*. When they are met, a person's motivation does *not* cease; instead, it increases and seeks further fulfillment. Therefore, the more success people achieve in their search for knowledge and understanding, the more likely they are to strive for even greater knowledge and understanding. Unlike deficiency needs, being needs can never be completely fulfilled. The motivation to achieve them is endlessly renewed.

This theory offers a way of looking at the adolescent as a whole, as a person whose physical, emotional, and intellectual needs are interrelated. Maslow's work has important implications for those working with adolescents. Kids who come to school or to programs hungry, sick, or hurt are unlikely to be motivated to seek knowledge and understanding. An adolescent whose feelings of safety and whose sense of belonging are threatened by a parental divorce under way at home, for instance, may have little interest in learning and exploring leadership skills. If a classroom or community center is a fearful, unpredictable place and adolescents seldom know where they stand, they are likely to be more concerned with security than with learning.

Maslow's hierarchy provides other insights into teen behavior. Adolescents' desires to fill lower-level needs may at times conflict with a teacher's and agency staff's desire to have them achieve higher-level goals. Belonging to a social group and maintaining self-esteem within that group, for example, is important to teens. If doing what the teacher says conflicts with group rules, adolescents may choose to ignore the teacher's wishes or even defy the teacher.

Awareness of adolescents' struggles to meet their needs provides a frame of reference within which to work. Interestingly, adolescents can and do demonstrate their leadership abilities during their fight to fulfill their needs. Helping them understand how they use their skills to meet their needs is part of helping them develop their potential.

Who's in Charge? The Struggle for Control

We have also come to appreciate adolescents' struggles to gain a sense of control over their lives. Rotter's concept of *locus of control* (1954) provides some additional insights into how to work with adolescents as they develop their leadership potential. Locus of control deals with *where* people locate responsibility for success and failure: inside or outside of themselves. As shown in Figure 2.2, locus of control captures the distinction between self-determination and control by others. For example, some people have an internal locus of control and so believe that they are responsible for their own fates. They like to work in situations where skill and effort can lead to success. Other people have an external locus of control, generally believing that people and forces outside of themselves control their fate. These individuals prefer to work in situations where luck determines the outcome of their lives.

Locus of control can be influenced by the behavior of others. Discrimination against women, people of color, and individuals with special needs can affect these individuals' perceptions of their own ability to control their lives. If people feel that they are not in control of their own lives, their self-esteem is likely to be diminished.

Ted, for instance, is a fifteen-year-old boy who has an external locus of control. He believes he has no control over what the future

Figure 2.2 Locus of Control

Internal	→	"What I do will make a big difference in what happens."
External	→	"No matter what I do, I cannot make a difference."

may bring. He thinks that no matter what he does, nothing will change for him unless fate or someone more powerful than himself comes along to make that difference. Ted doesn't participate in any school or community activities. He goes home after school and spends the better part of his time watching television.

Another adolescent, Tammy, is on the other end of the spectrum. She believes that she has the power to change all things by how she behaves. She is involved in many activities and is continually placed in leadership positions.

These are examples of opposite extremes. They are two very dissimilar individuals who are not differentiated by intelligence, socioeconomic status, race, or any other common way in which we identify people, but rather by locus of control.

In many ways, it is a mystery why some young people switch from an external locus of control in childhood to a more internal locus of control as they pass through adolescence. Research has found that an internal locus of control is correlated with many socially desirable variables, such as taking responsibility for one's own actions, being independent, exhibiting greater self-control, and staying in school (Lefcourt, 1966). Studies have shown (Chubb and Fertman, 1992) that locus of control is directly related to an individual's sense of belonging to his family. When an individual perceives his family as warm and inclusive, his internal locus of control is strengthened. When the opposite is true, an individual perceives his family as cold and detached, and his external locus of control is strengthened.

Helping adolescents develop their leadership abilities can have a direct impact on their locus of control. Strong leadership skills place an adolescent in charge of his or her life. Many adolescents don't feel that they are in charge of their lives, and getting older doesn't necessarily change this perception. Therefore, it is critical throughout the process of leadership development to help adolescents feel that they are in control and are able to make decisions that will influence their own lives and the lives of others.

Right and Wrong

In this book, we define leaders as those individuals (adult or adolescent) who think for themselves, communicate their thoughts and feelings to others, and help others understand and act on their own beliefs; they influence others in an ethical and socially responsible way. So in our work with adolescents, we have taken the time to look at teenagers' moral development. Working with adolescents in regard to ethics and social responsibility can be quite challenging. Most teens want to do the right thing, but they are frequently not sure what the right thing is. Especially with television glorifying violence, and with drugs and alcohol the popular means of pursuing fame and fortune, concepts such as family and community are being transformed, making distinctions between right and wrong, good and bad ever more blurred.

One useful source for understanding how adolescents develop their sense of right and wrong is the work of Lawrence Kohlberg (1963, 1975, 1981). He suggests that adolescents pass through a sequence of stages of judgment about right and wrong. We have divided moral reasoning development into three levels, as shown in Figure 2.3.

Kohlberg evaluated the moral reasoning of adolescents by presenting them with moral dilemmas, hypothetical situations in which people had to make difficult decisions. Study participants were asked what they thought the person caught in the dilemma should do, and they were asked to explain their answers. In these situations there were no obvious answers; no action would provide a complete solution. By the answers they gave, Kohlberg was able to gain insight into the development of adolescents' moral reasoning.

Figure 2.3 Stages of Moral Development

Stage 1	Judgment is based solely on a person's own needs and perceptions.
Stage 2	Expectations of society and law are taken into account.
Stage 3	Judgments are based on abstract personal principles that are not necessarily defined by society's laws.

Moral reasoning is related to both cognitive and emotional development. Abstract thinking becomes increasingly important in the higher stages of moral development, as adolescents move away from decisions based on absolute rules and toward decisions based on such principles as justice and mercy. The ability to see another's perspective and to imagine alternatives to existing laws and rules also affects judgments at the higher stages of development.

Kohlberg's work highlights the fact that the development of moral reasoning is a process. This process takes place over time, with periods of new learning and relearning. Helping adolescents understand the concept of morality in terms of influencing others is therefore an important part of leadership development, requiring constant attention to ethics as an integral component of responsible leadership. We must emphasize ethical leadership both in an adolescent's personal and public life, as a leader in the school, community, workplace, or family.

Asking the Right Questions

Carol Gilligan's work on the subject of girls' ethics and morality adds yet another dimension to the theory of moral development. Gilligan's work suggested to us three levels of moral development (see Figure 2.4). At the first level, the individual asks what is best for herself when making decisions. At the second level, she asks, "Am I doing what others expect of me?" At the third, the individual considers herself and others at once. Gilligan's work is significant in that she traces gender differences in moral reasoning to different ways of viewing the self. Females define themselves in

Figure 2.4   Three Levels of Moral Development

Level 1	Caring for the self	What is best for me?
Level 2	Caring for others	Am I doing what others expect of me?
Level 3	Caring for the self and others	Can I be responsible for myself and others at the same time?

relation to others; from this comes a sense of responsibility of one person for another. Males, on the other hand, define themselves as separate from others; this assumption of separation highlights the need for rules to regulate the actions of one person with respect to another (Woolfolk, 1995, p. 83.)

Gilligan found that females adopt an *ethic of care*. They think of morality in terms of their responsibility to others and are therefore concerned with *doing* something to meet the needs of others. This is different from males, who tend to think of responsibility as *not doing* something that would infringe on the rights of others (Woolfolk, 1995, p. 83).

From Theory to Advocacy

The work of Maslow, Rotter, Kohlberg, and Gilligan deepens our appreciation of life as an adolescent. It provides us with some understanding of what motivates adolescents and determines the sense of control they have over their lives. It also shows us how adolescents develop their sense of right and wrong, and the role that gender differences play in their development. A lot happens during adolescence, and these theories help us frame the teenage years. The theoretical framework gives us an idea of what to expect when working to develop adolescents' leadership potential and abilities.

Recognizing Adolescents as Leaders

There are many potential places for us to intervene to help adolescents develop their leadership potential. In fact, there are so many that the prospect of intervention can be rather overwhelming. The first step in the process is an easy one, since it does not directly involve intervention. Initially, we should simply recognize that teenagers are developing their leadership potential and abilities. Then, when we do begin to intervene, we can encourage transformational and transactional leadership. However, this should only take place after we have considered the adolescents themselves: how they differ and how they are alike.

How Adolescents Differ

What makes one young person different from another? Three major variables frequently explored by researchers are *gender, ethnicity,* and *socioeconomic status.* To understand the development of individuals, it is important to study each of these categories. However, a thorough discussion of these issues could fill volumes and is beyond the scope of this book. Instead of diving into this pool of information, we have pinpointed what we feel are particularly relevant aspects of each of these categories and discussed them in relation to adolescence.

Gender

All adolescents are expected to be responsible, make decisions, plan for the future, and generally be more mature than children. In certain ways, however, the roles of males and females in our society differ. Being raised as a boy or a girl has significant bearing how an individual views his or her ability to be a leader. The dominant culture teaches boys at an early age that to be successful they must be strong, aggressive, competitive, and ambitious. In short, it promotes the stereotypical notion of who are leaders. Girls are given a variation of this message, wherein these same qualities are desirable but have limitations. If girls are strongly competitive or aggressive, for instance, they are seen as pushy. Therefore, the same qualities that in boys are seen as strengths become negative in girls if they are too evident. One explanation for this phenomenon is that girls are often expected to be followers instead of leaders. Being a leader is not associated with girls. It is certainly not true in all cases or circumstances, though, that leadership potential of girls is not championed.

Boys and girls alike struggle with their popularity, bodies, and turbulent emotions in adolescence. However, the primary concerns of the two gender groups are not the same. Important goals for most adolescent males are to be strong, intelligent, competitive, and athletic. Their self-esteem is based on being successful in these areas. Boys who are not strong, athletic, and bright don't fit easily into the traditional view of a successful adolescent male. When they don't match this stereotype, they also find it difficult to see themselves as leaders. Girls, on the other hand, are acting as leaders in their group when they go *against* the typical female stereotype. Adolescent girls tend to be much more concerned with their appearance than with the character traits that concern boys. This greater self-consciousness makes it harder for girls to stand out and take a leadership role, since their focus is on trying to conform to a perfect image rather than on being individuals.

With the majority of adolescents, girls have lower self-esteem than boys (Simmons and Blyth, 1987). Gilligan, who has conducted extensive research with adolescents, asserts that girls usually manage to get through childhood with their "voice" (1990). However, they frequently experience more serious setbacks during adolescence than boys. Epidemiological studies repeatedly cite adolescence as a time of psychological risk and heightened vulnerability for girls (Petersen, 1988; Minnesota Women's Fund, 1990; American Association of University Women, 1991). The AAUW reports that "What once seemed ordinary to girls—speaking, difference, anger, conflict, fighting, bad as well as good thoughts and feelings—now seem treacherous: laced with danger, a sign of imperfection, a harbinger of being left out, not chosen" (1991, pp. 32–33).

Ethnicity

Ricardo Garcia (1991) compares culture to an iceberg. One-third of the iceberg is visible; the rest is hidden and unknown. Adolescents have been raised in cultures that have given them many messages about their ability to become leaders. Some cultural messages are overt; for example, many Vietnamese parents expect their children to work hard and excel in school. Other cultural messages are covert: "like most girls, black girls are raised to assume the traditional female role of nurturing and child care, but they are also encouraged to be strong and self-sufficient and to expect to work outside the home—as have generations of black women before them" (Taylor, Gilligan, and Sullivan, 1995, p. 43).

The ability and motivation to express one's opinions as a leader are strongly tied to the cultural environments in which children grow up. The more dominant the culture in which the child is raised, the more strongly tied he or she will be to the mores of that culture. Those raised in a multicultural environment are more likely to have varying points of view.

Socioeconomic Status

Socioeconomic status is a term used to refer to degrees of wealth, power, and prestige. Studies years ago focused on the wealthy and powerful as leaders. Leaders came from certain families who groomed their young to take their rightful places as leaders of society. Children learned at an early age that they would be expected to act as leaders some day.

Socioeconomic status still remains a powerful force in the lives of teenagers. Poverty, health problems, and school failure are all highly correlated to an adolescent's socioeconomic status. This one factor can overpower other differences such as ethnicity and gender. For example, upper-class Anglo-Europeans, African Americans, and Hispanic Americans typically find that they have much more in common with each other than with lower-class individuals from their own ethnic groups (Woolfolk, 1995). The consequence of this phenomenon is that we commonly see differences in expectations of and attitudes toward leadership development among adolescents from different socioeconomic backgrounds.

Often the message to teenagers who live in poverty is that they can't be leaders. This is a dangerous and damaging attitude.

Commonalities Among Adolescents

As discussed above, there are various factors that can affect each individual adolescent's ability to lead. However, there are also many ways in which development is similar in all adolescents. All adolescents struggle with their desire to separate themselves from their parents at a time when "attention from teachers becomes less abundant, less personal, and more focused on academic performance" (Basic Behavioral Science Task Force of the National Mental Health Council, 1996). Adolescence is a formative time during which people develop their individuality and are interested in trying new things and learning new skills. Teenagers are not so rigidly formed that they cannot alter their way of looking at the world. They are gathered in schools where large groups can be supported in developing their leadership potential. Most important, leadership development programs that focus on adolescence give teens the rest of their lives to use their leadership skills: "The choices made and paths taken at adolescence have the potential to be pivotal, setting the course of educational and vocational direction. . . ." (Taylor, Gilligan, and Sullivan, 1995, p. 69).

An adolescent who is thirteen behaves very differently from one who is seventeen, even if the two have never thought about leadership development. Clearly, adolescents go through many changes during this four-year span. What is important to keep in mind is that whether people are thirteen, seventeen, or twenty-five years old, if their leadership potential is not developed, then opportunities are passing them by. Thoughtful leadership development helps individuals learn more from their experiences and formal training.

Adolescent leadership development happens gradually. In early adolescence, teenagers experiment with various ways of acting, thinking, and feeling. The only certain thing is that there is a great deal of energy going into this search for self.

A puzzling part of identifying and understanding the leadership development process in adolescents is the uncertainty of an adolescent's behavior. Just when you think they are maturing and becoming better able to think for themselves, they seem to regress. One example is Lucy, who was very capable in her baby-sitting job. She was able to schedule times for activities and was very good at setting limits both for the children and herself. When it came to scheduling her own activities, however, Lucy was unable to set the guidelines she needed and then adhere to them. She did what most of us do, that is, perform very well in one aspect of her life but not so well in others.

Recognizing the leadership potential in every adolescent means accepting adolescence as a time of exploration. Adults who work with adolescents must constantly remind themselves that young people face many obstacles in maximizing their potential. Being aware of established developmental theory can help adults facilitate the process of leadership development. When adolescents experiment with their growing sense of individuality, the outward signs can take many forms. Adults struggle with adolescents when they are in this stage of identity-seeking because the teenagers are beginning to make choices with little or no advice from authority figures.

Because leadership takes so many different forms, identifying and supporting leadership behaviors is difficult. As we have said repeatedly, adolescents often receive messages from the adults in their lives and from the communities around them that impede them in fully realizing their leadership potential.

Chapter Three

How Adolescents Acquire Leadership Skills

We believe that leadership development is experienced by individuals as a continuing process. In the adolescent period, leadership development is best viewed as proceeding in three stages (awareness, interaction, and mastery). Each stage comprises a group of behaviors that generally show a progression toward more advanced uses of leadership ability. As teens become aware of the knowledge they already possess, they are able to use it to make decisions that match their needs. Even though each adolescent is unique, he or she also has certain things in common with other teens at every stage. Advancement through the stages starts and stops; teens move back and forth between stages as they try out different ways to fulfill their needs and desires. In each stage, adolescents address aspects of transformational and transactional leadership. The balance between performing leadership tasks and being a leader varies as well. However, both aspects of leadership must be explored and developed before an adolescent's leadership potential can be fully realized.

Dimensions of the Leadership Development Stages

From our past research (Fertman and Long, 1990; Fertman and Chubb, 1993; Wald and Pringle, 1995; Long, Wald, and Graf, 1996), we have identified five dimensions found within each leadership development stage:

1. Leadership information

2. Leadership attitude

3. Communication

4. Decision making

5. Stress management

The dimensions encompass cognitive, emotional, and behavioral aspects. They provide a consistent frame of reference to assess, monitor, and evaluate an adolescent's leadership development. They also offer adults who interact with teenagers concrete guidelines for understanding and supporting the development of leadership in adolescents. As a means of highlighting both transformational and transactional aspects of leadership development throughout the process, we further subdivide each dimension. The dimensions of each stage are shown in Figure 3.1.

Leadership Information

Leadership information—what adolescents know about leaders and leadership—is the first dimension found in all the leadership development stages. Accurate information is critical to leadership development. Although it is not sufficient to stimulate leadership behavior on its own, it plays a central role in adolescents' choices concerning leadership. Sources of information are as plentiful and diverse as the people teens know, the myriad experiences they have had, the publications they read, and the programs they attend. Adolescents are bombarded with a mass of information every day, though only a small portion of it remains with them and is understood. The information may be ignored; it may be acknowledged, but still not remain; it may be retained for a short time and then be forgotten; or indeed it may remain, only to be disbelieved or redefined. The aim, then, is to present information in a way that is attractive and has immediate appeal to teens, thus enabling it to be accepted and retained. The first and perhaps most difficult challenge for adults and adolescents alike, then, is to make sense of all the leadership information available.

Figure 3.1 Dimensions of a Leadership Development Stage

	Transformational	*Transactional*
Leadership information		
Leadership attitude		
Communication skills		
Decision-making skills		
Stress-management skills		

Teens are constantly receiving, processing, sorting, storing, retrieving, and discarding information about leadership and leaders. Adults who work with adolescents can help them facilitate a discriminating search for pertinent information, while ensuring that it is available in a friendly format, useful (in other words, that it is what a teen wants to know), and processable (within reach of the teen's time, energy, and comprehension level). Often, information is exaggerated and leads adolescents to incorrect conclusions, or even to a fatalistic attitude that leadership is not for them. There is a danger of going to the other extreme as well. In our desire to make sense of a complex world, we have a tendency to oversimplify leadership information. If teens are to trust this information, it must be valid and reliable.

Leadership Attitude

Leadership attitude is the second dimension. It refers to adolescents' dispositions, thoughts, and feelings (both positive and negative) toward identifying themselves as leaders. A teenager's leadership attitude predisposes him or her to lead. Adolescent attitudes toward leadership are learned; they do not magically appear as a person matures physically. These attitudes are acquired through direct instruction, by taking on the viewpoints of someone who is loved or admired (identification) or by adopting a social role as, for example, a pupil-teacher, athlete, or camp counselor. Attitude change is the acquisition, reversal, or intensification of an attitude; during adolescence an individual's attitudes are continuously open to modification and change.

Attitudes are constantly altered according to the adolescent's experience. Both the original learning and the modification of an attitude take place through interactions with other people. Inter-action can be direct (occurring in person) or indirect (through movies, advertisements, books, television, and so on). However, it is *always* within systems of human relationships that adolescent attitudes are learned and modified. The acquiring and modifying of attitudes, then, is a dynamic process in which other people con-front adolescents with expectations about "appropriate" attitudes at a time when teenagers are struggling to increase their compe-tence in dealing with their environment by seeking attitudes that help make sense of the world around them.

Teenagers are not passive learners. They select the things they do or do not pay attention to, and they choose how to respond to the demands of parents, teachers, and peers. Adolescents strive to for-mulate individual viewpoints, weighing those attitudes against the expectations of others, both adults and peers, who have their own opinions about which ideas and behaviors are appropriate. These forces are in a dynamic state of either tension or equilibrium in which an accommodation is reached, thus forming the teenager's attitude.

Communication Skills

Communication—the exchange of thoughts, messages, and infor-mation—is the third dimension of the leadership development stages. It is the process of sharing knowledge, interests, attitudes, opinions, feelings, and ideas with others. It is through communica-tion that one person influences another. The process of communi-cation can include both verbal and nonverbal messages. Successful communication depends on mutual understanding of the sender and receiver. Communication is not just a matter of saying some-thing, and it is not a matter of luck; it requires skill. Like any skill, the ability to communicate with competence must be learned and developed over a lifetime. Communication is a critical talent for leaders. As one authority stated in his work on leadership development, "If I had to name a single, all-purpose instrument of leadership it would be communication . . . [and] most of the communication necessary for leadership can be taught" (Gardner, 1987, p. 13).

Communication skills are a fundamental part of leadership because they permit the flow of ideas from one individual to another or to a group, and vice versa. Effective communication helps adolescents break down barriers between themselves and others, and between themselves and adults in particular. Giving careful thought not only to *what* they want to express but also to *how* they want to express it is often a new concept for adolescents.

A good place to start with leadership development is to break down the components of communication, since all other skills in some way build on communication. Communication consists of three things: sending, receiving, and responding to a message. The sender must deliver a clear message, taking into consideration the characteristics of the individual(s) receiving the message. Is the person a child, or an adult? Is there one person, or are there twenty? These and similar factors all determine how the message should be sent. Next, the message is received. It is important to remember that receivers translate what they hear based on their own set of definitions, which may differ greatly from those of the sender. The final component of communication is response. A response lets the sender know that the message has been received. All three parts are necessary for effective communication.

Nonverbal messages are also an important aspect of communication. If 60 percent of the messages sent, received, or responded to are nonverbal, then it is very important to be aware of nonverbal messages and to be able to read the nonverbal signals of others. The relationship between verbal and nonverbal communication is important. If what is being said matches a person's body language and tone of voice, then the message is congruent. Congruent messages imply credibility.

A receiver interprets a message based on his or her own background and conditioning. In other words, a receiver sees and hears what he or she has been conditioned and trained to see and hear. The receiver gives meaning to the sender's message and then responds to these interpretations. The meaning interpreted by the receiver may or may not be the message's intended meaning. For this reason, both the sender and receiver must make an effort to be clear and accurate when they communicate. Communication skills provide teenagers with the basic tools they need to make contact with each other and work toward achieving day-to-day goals. Communication seems simple in theory; it appears, to a large degree, to be performed without much thought. But this is not the case. Communication involves a complex interaction of habits, attitudes, knowledge, information, and bias. What adolescents say, how they say it, and how they react to what others say are all determined by their own complex communication system.

Decision-Making Skills

Decision making (choosing between competing courses of action) is the fourth dimension. Decision making is what leadership is all about; it is making choices that influence others in an ethical and socially responsible way. As adolescents become more autonomous, they are required to make more of their own decisions. In doing so, they cope with the conflicting demands of parents, school, peers, and work. Adolescents in all stages of leadership development already have considerable knowledge and intuitively approach decision making. A key difference between transformational and transactional leadership is precisely in this decision-making process. Transformational leaders take into account input from everyone involved and then make decisions. Transactional leaders make decisions based on their own ideas and beliefs—even if everyone has not been heard—in order to move forward.

According to most general models of decision making (Raiffa, 1968; von Winterfeldt and Edwards, 1986), a person facing a decision should (1) list possible alternatives, (2) identify the potential consequences of those actions, (3) assess the probability of each consequence occurring if the relevant action were undertaken, (4) assess the relative impact (positive or negative) of each consequence, and (5) evaluate these impacts and probabilities to identify the most attractive course of action. People who follow these steps are said to behave rationally. Those who can follow the steps effectively are said to behave optimally. Therefore, a person can act rationally by following the steps, even if she does so without much success. It would be an overwhelming task to translate the process into terms that enable adolescents to use this paradigm for each decision they make. A more modest (and more common) approach is to teach teenagers the basic principles involved, with the knowledge that their consciousness of the process may provoke some forethought, which results in better decisions.

Stress-Management Skills

Stress management—how adolescents react to and deal with the stress in their lives—is the fifth dimension of the leadership development stages. Stress is not easy to define. Most teenagers readily talk about being stressed out, burned out, and overloaded. Researchers, on the other hand, often have difficulty defining stress in scientific terms. In one definition, stress is described as the level at which a person's internal resources are taxed or exceeded by the external environment. In other words, stress is any physiological response of the body to demands from the external environment (people, situations, elements), internal mental processes (worry, fear, happiness), or physiological processes (drugs, blood sugar, biorhythms). This physiological arousal is generally called the "stress response." A stressor triggers the stress response; it can be an emotional experience, an intellectual challenge, a social situation, a spiritual epiphany, an environmental pollutant, or a physical stimulant. However, there is much more to understanding stress than simply studying physiological reactions. To be able to predict how teenagers will react to stress, we must have information about their personalities, their physical makeup, their perceptions, and the context in which the stress occurs (Hobfoll, 1988). The multiple facets involved in evaluating stress, including physiological, psychological, and social reactions, must all be studied to paint a clear picture of adolescent stress responses.

We view stress, for the most part, as a positive element in adolescents' lives; management of stress should be approached positively. It is important that teenagers not be stressed to the point that their behavior becomes counterproductive or they become physically ill. Teenagers have a repertoire of coping strategies to deal with stress, some effective and some ineffective. An important point about effective coping strategies is that adolescents can often use more than one at a time to help them deal with stress. Stress management involves many stressors, but one that stands out for us is the stress that adolescents associate with their developing leadership potential. There is much anxiety involved in dealing with the consequences of the choices one makes as a leader. The ability of adolescents to regulate this stress influences their performance as leaders.

Leadership Interactions: People, Activities, Learning Experience

Leadership is a social process; it happens among people. Teenagers are constantly learning and relearning about themselves and others as leaders. Two serious drawbacks in the current approach to leadership development are its limited focus and its low visibility to many young people (as we explored in Chapter One). Because of these shortcomings, most teenagers don't think about leadership. For this to change, both adolescents and adults need to make conscious decisions to pursue leadership in their lives.

One way to start fostering this consciousness is for us to look at how youths can and do learn about leadership. These are the points presented in Figure 3.2. We argue in this book that it is at these

Figure 3.2 Leadership Development Interactions

	Family	Community	School	Work
People	Parents, siblings, grandparents, cousins, aunts and uncles	Neighbors, youth organization staff members, clergy, employers, community leaders	Teachers, counselors, principals, peers, nurses, coaches	Supervisors, coworkers, clients, customers
Activities	Chores, vacations, hobbies, holidays, family celebrations	Lessons, clubs, sports, youth groups, volunteering	Clubs, sports, class discussions and presentations, student government, service clubs	Finding a job, interviewing, performing job duties
Learning Experience	Baby-sitting for younger siblings, cooking meals, visits to the library	Scout training, YMCA/YWCA and other associations, Red Cross, leadership camp	Sports, clubs, training for class office, leadership classes	Orientation, on-the-job training, supervision, apprenticeship

points of intervention that we often miss opportunities to help teenagers develop their leadership potential and abilities. These opportunities are interactions between people, activities, and learning; they are found across the spectrum of adolescents' families, communities, schools, and workplaces.

People

Family	Community	School	Work
Parents, siblings, grandparents, cousins, aunts and uncles	Neighbors, youth organization staff members, clergy, employers, community leaders	Teachers, counselors, principals, peers, nurses, coaches	Supervisors, coworkers, clients, customers

Leadership is a social process. Being a leader involves interacting with people; it cannot be done in isolation. Other people are always an essential source of guidance. We all remember the parent we looked to for advice and support, the special teacher who managed to excite us about learning, the coach who inspired us to do our best, or the first employer who taught us about the working world. People serve as role models, mentors, and peers. They are our sponsors and support systems. Teenagers learn to be leaders by watching the people around them act as leaders. Leadership is learned by watching, imitating, and practicing with people. It involves trial and error and learning from mistakes and successes alike.

We do not need to have a relationship with people to learn from them. What we learn from outside role models can be as valuable as knowledge gained from teachers, friends, coaches, siblings, and parents. Many of us look to historical figures or to well-known contemporary leaders for inspiration and learning. Frequently these are transformational leaders, who provide model examples of leadership.

Family. The family is the first organized group within which we witness displays of leadership. In this environment, adults are the leaders. As parents take leadership roles, children observe who undertakes each task and how they get things done. Children learn how to have an impact on their family system. The parents' (or caretakers') style can be democratic, authoritarian, or somewhere between the two. Children watch and learn how to behave and then begin to practice their own leadership skills. Young children are very self-centered, believing that the world revolves around them. Self-leadership for them means getting what they want. Adult leadership involves determining what is required to keep the child safe and growing. This is the early stage of leadership development. As children mature, they begin to understand that rules are not always arbitrary; they find that rules can be useful and often ensure their safety. If the environment is such that the child feels comfortable voicing his opinions and making decisions that are appropriate to his level of maturity, then the child begins to measure his ability to have an influence on his world.

Family members are role models for each other's leadership development. When children and teenagers see their parents participating in community activities, serving on boards for community-based organizations, or assisting with recreational and sports programs, they are likely to want to be involved in such activities themselves. Brothers, sisters, and cousins guide our development by setting expectations for how they think we should behave, and by providing us with feedback as we grow and develop. Children are often strongly influenced in their development by an older sibling's behavior, either because of a desire to emulate that sibling—to follow in her footsteps—or a desire to be different, thus making a statement of individuality. A person's family sets expectations for behavior and leadership early in life.

Community. For children, the community is only as large as their immediate and tangible surroundings. As they mature into adolescents, however, they gain the ability to think more abstractly and have a sense of community with people who are half a world away. Moving into late childhood and early adolescence, they become more open to the wider community and to a variety of different people: friends, relatives, neighbors, clergy, community youth workers, and business and civic leaders. All of these people are essential sources of guidance and feedback for youths.

How do adolescents define their community? For early adolescents, it often means neighbors, schoolmates, teammates in sports, and club members (Figure 3.3). For older adolescents, the definition probably includes more adults, such as parents of friends, other adult friends, and perhaps a boss (Figure 3.4). These adults often become role models for adolescents who are beginning to formulate their own set of ethics and values. Adolescents learn from watching how these influential people deal with situations and assert their leadership skills.

Community members' attitudes and behavior in relation to leadership development for adolescents provides the stage and backdrop for that development. Children and adolescents usually

Figure 3.3 Levels of Community for
Ten-to-Fourteen-Year-Olds

Family

Extended family (if nearby)

Friends or neighbors on the street or in the
apartment building

Classmates and peers

Teammates and club members

Teachers

People who have had direct contact with the adolescent

know little about the formal leadership in their community, but they intuitively know who has power in their community. They know the issues that are important in the community, and who is or is not addressing those issues. They know the opportunities for them to participate in community politics, activities, and special events. Messages about the role of girls and boys as leaders are very strong within a community. The sources of these messages are not only people the children know but the media—which are full of contentious images about leadership and leaders. What is typically learned from the community and the media is a stereotype about leadership and leaders.

School. School is the place were youths begin to learn how to behave in groups outside their family. In school, the teachers are the leaders. Children and adolescents learn a lot about leadership from their teachers. Teachers set the tone in classrooms, make the environment safe, offer support, and provide guidance for students. Teachers are also challenged and tested by students; students witness a teacher's ability to control and direct a class. They make judgments about what they like and dislike about a teacher— which can in turn shape their behavior and thinking about how the students themselves might direct a class if given the chance.

School principals are also leaders. Most youths associate prin-

**Figure 3.4 Levels of Community for
Fifteen-to-Nineteen-Year-Olds**

Family

Extended family (if nearby)

Neighborhood friends, classmates, friends from
other schools, friends from far away

Teammates, club members, older or
younger friends

Teachers and counselors

Boss and coworkers

Community police or firefighters

Elected community officials

cipals with authority; they have power and make decisions that affect the lives of young people. In many cases, the principal is someone a child wants to avoid; in itself this is a statement of the way children view leadership and authority. We want to encourage young people to know leaders, not shy away from them.

Beyond teachers and principals, there are counselors, nurses, bus drivers, support personnel, activity directors, and coaches all actively involved with leadership development. These individuals often have the opportunity to develop individual relationships with students that can support the leadership development process.

As children approach early adolescence, peers begin to have a much stronger influence on their behavior and attitudes. School is where teenagers have the greatest contact with peers. Groups of friends are the adolescent's lifeblood. They provide the acceptance that is necessary for young people to feel that they belong. Before further development can take place, adolescents must establish groups of friends.

Older adolescents are models for younger adolescents. They can make an impact on young adolescents that is not so readily available to adults. This is seldom apparent to older adolescents; however, when they are made aware of their influence and are properly trained, they can be highly effective teachers.

Work.   Most people have their first job experience during adolescence. They work after school, on the weekends, and during the summer. The people whom adolescents meet at their first job become models for how a person should behave in the world of work. Bosses, coworkers, clients, and customers help define the kind of behavior a job requires. If expectations are clear, most adolescents find the work rewarding, and not just in the extrinsic sense. Accomplishing a task that is different from those at home or at school, and being paid for it, is to adolescents an important aspect of a job. It is a step into the adult world that is both exciting and scary. Adolescents learn new rules and roles at work, hastening their departure from childhood.

Bosses are extremely important as sources of performance feedback and as role models. The best employers are those who challenge teenagers, trust them, are consistent in their behavior, and are willing to spend time with adolescents. Like all other leaders, bosses must be credible if teenagers are to learn from them. It is best if a boss has these qualities of challenging, trusting, and being available, but even a negative boss is not necessarily a roadblock to development. Such a person can create unwanted stress and may not be pleasant to work with, but at the least she provides an excellent example of what *not* to do.

Coworkers can also be excellent models during an adolescent's formative years. Observing how older and more experienced coworkers accomplish their tasks and how they feel about their work—their attitudes about their job—provides a foundation in adolescents for their own attitudes about future work. Peers at work provide teenagers with a different view of the workplace and with further models of how to behave. They also provide teenagers with a support network that can be helpful at school, in the community, and at future jobs.

The workplace is where many parents spend much of their time. Children and adolescents may not be able to describe their parents' jobs in great detail, but they generally have some idea of the tasks their parents perform at work, the amount of schooling their parents completed to get the job, and whether their parents are supervisors, bosses, administrators, or staff members. During adolescence, discussing work helps teens begin to think about their futures. It is frequently during such talks that adolescents first declare that they want to do something special, that is, in some sense they want to be a leader. In concrete terms, they may express a desire to be a business owner, a professional with a private practice, an officer in the armed services, or a police detective, and so on. What we hear from teenagers in discussions about future careers is that they want to influence people and make a difference. They want to be leaders.

Activities

Family	Community	School	Work
Chores, vacations, hobbies, holidays, family celebrations	Lessons, clubs, sports, youth groups, volunteering	Clubs, sports, class discussions and presentations, student government, service clubs	Finding a job, interviewing, performing job duties

In activities, teenagers practice being leaders. Even though many activities are initiated through schools, community agencies and youth-serving organizations are another large potential resource for development of leadership activities and opportunities. Activities can range from formal lessons with a private teacher to neighborhood sports leagues staffed with community volunteers.

Activities provide real-life situations within which adolescents can learn more about their leadership skills while being guided by adult support and structure. This is experiential learning, learning by doing. Not just any experience, however, supports individual development. Activities that develop leadership must be challenging, providing teenagers with opportunities to test themselves against new and difficult tasks. Adolescents need a range of activities to broaden their base of experience. Exposure to various groups and activities provides them with opportunities to test their skills in different environments and with different people. These kinds of activities can indeed be the best teachers.

The true value of activities in relation to leadership development is that they provide adolescents with fuel for thought. After participating in activities, young people must be given a chance to reflect on what they have learned. Activities provide the structure for adolescents to practice reflection. During these periods of reflection, teenagers carefully consider what they think. They meditate, muse, contemplate, ponder, deliberate, cogitate, reason, and speculate. Reflection involves asking oneself "What am I doing and why?" "What am I learning?" "Am I acting as a leader?" Reflection is a means of assessing one's behavior and satisfaction or dissatisfaction with that behavior. In reflecting, adolescents acquire insights that allow them to build on their strengths and set goals in areas where they know they need further development. Reflection also offers adults who work with youths an opportunity to identify an adolescent's level of leadership development. Adolescents are not always provided with time to reflect; but without some time to think about what they have learned in an activity, the long-term benefits of that activity are diminished.

Family. Children and adolescents learn to act as leaders as they participate with their families in activities. Such activities vary from the purely informal to the ritualistic. They include vacations; public services; holiday celebrations; organized club and religious celebrations, meetings, or events; and academic, artistic, athletic, vocational, and health-related activities. These activities provide an environment where leadership and social competence can develop. Through these experiences, individuals learn to use their resources in various environments. Participation in leadership opportunities through such activities prepares young people to transfer their skills to other areas of their lives.

There are many adolescents who do not experience organized family activities that focus on developing leadership abilities, but such development does take place even without this focus. Youths involved with any sort of group learn about their place within that group (despite any lack of discussion on the subject). This is where leadership patterns are set for life. Adolescents learn about rules and regulations very early on; if they adhere to the rules they do not get into trouble, but if they do not follow them, their fate is much less certain. When adolescents are guided to reflect on the rules they have learned, it is then possible for them to question and develop a set of rules based on their own beliefs.

Families that take the time to reflect on their activities—when they ask questions, make suggestions, and communicate effectively—can further positive leadership development. Parents or caregivers are role models who help form adolescents' attitudes and dictate ethical and responsible behavior toward others.

Community. Is the community interested in its young people? What kinds of opportunities are available for youth and community to interact? Many communities have active sports teams for young people; this is often the first place where children get to interact with their community. Participating in such activities, they get to know adults other than their parents. Leadership development takes place during all community activities.

Community members may gather together for many different reasons. Each community has its own personality and character. A community in Montana may come together on the Fourth of July for a fair or a rodeo, with participation or attendance by almost every person within a fifty-mile radius. A neighborhood in Pittsburgh, on the other hand, may have a tradition of an annual block party where the immediate neighborhood gathers to cook food and play games. Youths learn about leadership by participating in all of these activities.

Church youth groups are another community gathering place where teens learn to use their leadership skills. The combination of religious education and social events provides important support for a family's belief system. Youth groups often participate in service projects for the community, and this offers young people a closer look at the needs of their community.

Some communities are full of opportunities to take lessons outside of school. Children may start lessons at a very young age, studying music, dance, martial arts, or gymnastics. Such experiences provide exposure to people outside of the kids' families; they are all important in the development of leadership ability.

Through these activities, young people form a closer relationship with the community around them and learn about leadership by observing adult interactions within a group. Is the interaction "top down"? That is, who takes charge among the adolescents? Do the adults choose an adolescent to lead? How good are the teens at each activity? How do they handle success and failure? Whether they are aware of their knowledge or not, adolescents learn the answers to these questions by observing the actions and interactions of those around them and by participating themselves in group activities. If community activities are not available, or are not taken advantage of, then many opportunities for learning about leadership are missed.

School. Activities vary greatly from school to school. Some are institutions (in the sense that student council, for instance, has been a part of schools for many years). Others are new and struggle to maintain their membership rolls. As youths progress through school, the number and variety of activities in the school increase. In all of these activities, teens can practice interacting with peers and adults on a level different from that in the classroom. School activities provide both positive and negative learning experiences. Negative experiences can often be more effective teachers than positive ones—if the adolescents understand that it is okay to fail. Depending on the school district, resources and support for school activities can be extensive or they can be minimal. Many schools have activity directors, who organize and coordinate school activities. Listed in Figure 3.5 are some of the more traditional activities found in high schools. But they are by no means the only ones available; many schools offer volunteer opportunities, class trips, schoolwide activities, and art shows. All school activities offer teenagers easy access to groups of peers who share similar interests, material and equipment resources, and adult supervision. The potential for leadership development through school activities is quite high if a school takes advantage of the opportunity such activities offer.

Work. Jobs can provide many opportunities for adolescents to develop leadership skills by way of activity. It may be difficult for them to take advantage of such opportunities, however, since it is often the case that teenagers are hired to do jobs that require minimal skills and little creativity. Adolescents frequently find their job boring, make poor decisions, and end up leaving after a relatively short period of time (anywhere from a few days to a few weeks). However, each step of this process—from deciding to get a job to searching, interviewing, and reporting to work—provides opportunities for adolescents to think about who they are and how they fit into the working world.

Activities related to finding a job can often be confusing for adolescents. Completing applications, getting a social security number, and getting a work permit are all part of this process. At the time they begin their job search, most adolescents have already

Figure 3.5 School Activities That Provide Leadership Opportunities

Sports teams: varsity, intramural	Service organizations: Key Club
Team support: cheerleaders, pep clubs	Honor societies
Language clubs	Game clubs: chess, computer
Drama: play productions	Newspaper and yearbook
Future professions: Future Business Leaders of America, Future Farmers of America	Student council, class officers, peer mentors
School help: office, library, teacher	Music: chorus, stage, marching band

performed some sort of informal work, perhaps baby-sitting or cutting grass for the neighbors. Even though these experiences offer a small preview of what it is like to be in the working world, the first official job can be a rite of passage for an adolescent. After finding work, an adolescent must figure out how to manage his or her time so that the job doesn't interfere with other responsibilities at home and at school.

Learning Experience

Family	Community	School	Work
Baby-sitting for younger siblings, cooking meals, visits to the library	Scout training, YMCA/YWCA and other associations, Red Cross, leadership camp	Sports, clubs, training for class office, leadership classes	Orientation, on-the-job training, supervision, apprenticeship

By *learning experiences* we mean educational programs that focus on leadership either directly or indirectly. Regardless of the adolescents involved (be they class officers, middle school students, or sports teammates), the stated purpose of the experience, the geographical area served, or the duration of the program, experiences that directly address leadership development usually have a similar goal: to provide leadership information, encourage teenagers to think about themselves as leaders, and improve some subset of the participants' leadership skills. Typically, these experiences are a mix of lectures and small-group or large-group activities that focus on topics such as recruiting participants, planning projects, public speaking, and leading meetings. Recently, a growing number of youth experiences such as Outward Bound have focused on adolescents' working in groups and learning to influence others.

Learning experiences that indirectly address leadership are those programs and activities that recognize and celebrate leadership but whose intent is not primarily to educate youth about their leadership potential and abilities. Examples of such a program are school assemblies for Martin Luther King, Jr.'s, birthday and Great Americans Day. Apprenticeships and internships are also indirect learning experiences. The challenge is to heighten adolescents' and adults' awareness of the knowledge to be gained from such activities, allowing reflection to make their learning more concrete.

The content of most learning experiences is not consciously based on empirical research, but it usually incorporates the findings of such research. This apparent fit between what the current literature recommends and what adolescents are actually taught may be more a function of intuition than the result of deliberate, knowledge-based planning on the part of program coordinators. Certain qualities are desirable in a learning experience that focuses directly on leadership development. For example, high-quality experiences are based on the needs and experience of the adolescents involved, differentiate between transformational and transactional leadership, offer students the opportunity to practice their skills, and ensure that all staff members are supervised and well trained. Figure 3.6 lists qualities that are desirable in a leadership learning experience.

Figure 3.6 Qualities of Leadership Learning Experiences

1. Learning experience is based on adolescents' needs and experience.
2. Definition of leadership includes both transactional and transformational leadership.
3. Purpose is clearly stated.
4. Curriculum and materials are researched and tested.
5. Student assessment and feedback are offered.
6. There are multiple opportunities to practice skills.
7. Learning methods vary (lecture, small group, audiovisual).
8. Follow-up and ongoing support are included.
9. Communication with schools, agencies, and families is emphasized.
10. Staff are well trained and supervised.

Family. There is very little formal learning experience in families, but there can be much informal learning experience that prepares and encourages young people to take on leadership roles outside the family circle. Sometimes adults premeditate a learning experience, giving that experience a process and a purpose; an example is preparing adolescents to take responsibility for meal preparation. Teenagers start by shopping and cooking with their parents, and then gradually take on more responsibility for the task. This can be thought of as an apprenticeship: learning at home by doing chores and working with other family members as a team. Sharing the responsibility of meaningful work in the family can go a long way toward leadership development.

Community. Direct opportunities for leadership development in the community often come through organized community programs. Scouting, YMCA/YWCA and other associations, the Red Cross, Boys and Girls Clubs, Campfire Boys and Girls, and many other such programs offer leadership training as part of their activities. These varied activities are for the most part excellent ways for adolescents to practice applying their leadership skills. Earning badges in scouting groups, for instance, can be an important learning experience. Working with groups of peers, younger kids, and adults offers a chance to try out new leadership roles.

School. Teenagers learn a lot of what they know about leadership through formal education and schooling. Starting in preschool and continuing through high school, assemblies, assignments, and classroom instruction are devoted to leadership studies. Of course, this instruction isn't called that, but in every subject area students learn about people who were leaders and study the past actions and accomplishments of these individuals. In U.S. history, students learn about the people who were responsible for setting our country's vision and making critical decisions about its formation. In science, they learn about men and women whose scientific investigations led to important discoveries. In art, students learn about the great masters and the influence their work has on art even today. One unwanted consequence of this focus in schools is that students develop stereotypical ideas about who leaders are and consequently start to doubt their own leadership abilities.

Students who are already active in formal school activities frequently have opportunities to attend formal leadership training. This training might occur as part of their regular school activities. For example, a teacher who sponsors the student council may conduct a leadership training session for all student council members as part of council orientation. The National Association of Secondary School Principals has a formal leadership development program for high school students that many schools use as part of student council training. Organizations such as the Hugh O'Brian Youth Foundation operate leadership development workshops for high schools. Unfortunately, we have found that for students not involved in formal school activities, opportunities for leadership education are limited.

Work. Most work situations offer many opportunities for both direct and indirect leadership learning experience. Starting with orientation, on-the-job training and supervision, and apprenticeship, adolescents learn not only the kinds of responsibilities a job entails but also the personal requirements necessary for the job. If youths are dealing directly with the public, then they need to learn from adults what behavior is appropriate with such individuals. In all cases, adolescents need to be given the opportunity to ask questions about required responsibilities and behavior. A formal, paying job is a new circumstance for most adolescents, and with this unaccustomed drain on their time they must learn how to balance and organize other areas of their lives. This sometimes presents problems, because they are often not the only ones who have a hand in scheduling their time. It may be that parental and school schedules take precedence over the adolescent's job.

More and more teens are in the workforce today. They make and spend more money than they ever have before. Early work experience helps them develop lifelong saving and spending patterns that will influence their behavior and choices later in life. Such responsibility teaches valuable leadership skills that cannot be learned in any situation fabricated in a classroom or program activity. Experiencing the workplace-as-teacher has the advantage of offering a real-life situation with very real consequences for both positive and negative behavior.

This chapter has laid a foundation for understanding our stage-oriented approach to adolescent leadership development. We have discussed the dimensions within these stages, which concentrate on specific areas that we have learned are critical to the development of leadership. The perspective on adolescents and leadership offered here is a framework to help adults organize their thinking and plan a course of action to help young people fully develop their potential.

As we have said before, no one framework or system is foolproof, but having one that is fluid and adaptable enables us to learn more. Although this lack of a concrete formula may frustrate adults, it also allows for a more complete comprehension and appreciation of what each individual brings to the process. Expanding our thinking about where leadership learning happens in families, schools, workplaces, and communities helps us recognize and support the needs of youth.

Part Two

Stages of Leadership Development

We now discuss working with adolescents to develop their leadership potential. We illustrate each of the three stages of leadership development using a case study of an adolescent. Bob represents the first stage; leadership isn't part of his life. Katie, in stage two, is thinking about leadership; she is excited about being a leader and doing leadership tasks. Damian, in stage three, is focused and using his leadership skills and abilities to "step up."

The cases, which are composites drawn from several teenagers at each stage, are designed to help you decipher the different adolescent leadership information, attitudes, and behavior seen in each stage.

Movement between the stages is fluid. We have found that with guidance and support, adolescents make steady, consistent progress in their leadership development. For some youths, the progress is relatively linear; it is low-key, steady, and focused. For most, however, it's a creative process characterized by bursts of energy, insight, and activity followed by periods of rest, distraction, and reflection. Adolescents have the potential to develop and grow in many directions and areas; we believe that supporting leadership development in adolescents encourages this growth. It helps adolescents see themselves, and be seen by others, as leaders.

As part of the next three chapters, we offer suggestions on how to work with adolescents in each stage of leadership development. This gives adults who interact with teenagers concrete guidelines for understanding and supporting adolescent leadership development. We include information that focuses on both transformational and transactional leadership to maximize leadership program design, implementation, and evaluation.

Chapter Four

Stage One: Awareness

I'm not a leader.

—*Bob, ninth grade*

You can often see just by looking at young people that they don't believe in their leadership abilities. Adolescents in the awareness stage of leadership development don't think leadership is part of their lives. They're in school, hanging out with friends, sometimes working, often trying to decide what to do with their time after school, before they go home to dinner and an evening of telephone conversations, video games, chores, baby-sitting, television, family activities, and homework. Leadership seems distant. But it is actually found very close to these adolescents, once they are aware of it.

Bob

Bob was a student at Coron High School, one of 350 freshmen, most of whom were sons and daughters of steelworkers turned service workers, administrative assistants, and technicians. The effects of the downslide of the steel industry fifteen years ago still linger in the area; the district has definitely seen better days.

As for Bob, he melted in among his friends. They were a pack. They dressed alike, cut up on each other, and often laughed out loud; Bob was fourteen, tall, skinny, and shy around people he didn't know. He had two younger sisters, Sally and Lily, nine and eleven. He had at least one fight a day with each of them, mostly regarding which TV programs to watch. Bob spent most of his time playing video games and hanging out with two buddies, Frank and

Ramon. In the summer before his freshman year in high school, his parents decided that they would have to do something about the amount of time he spent with video games, so they got him involved with the summer youth basketball league. It met in the mornings; they sent him to the community pool in the afternoons. He liked to dive. He even thought about joining the high school swim team.

We got to know Bob during his freshman year. Up until that time, Bob hadn't shown any awareness that his leadership potential was already a part of him. Since Bob had never even heard of a class in leadership—it wasn't a subject like reading, science, or math—he had never really given it a thought. In middle school he wasn't active with an after-school activity or sports team. Nor was he a member of student council, a class representative, or a class officer. He was not a member of the honor society. He never made the honor role in middle school, but he did maintain decent grades, mostly B's and C's.

Bob believed that he had very little control over his world, and very little say in what happened in his life. He thought that something or somebody else made most of the decisions that affected him. Bob was right, in fact; his parents *did* made all of his major life decisions for him. As a result, he learned to depend on adults (his parents and teachers) to set standards and provide structures for him to follow. Even though he often did his best to avoid living totally within these standards and strictures, he unconsciously depended on them. Bob believed that he could not be responsible for creating the rules, but only for obeying them.

At the same time, like most adolescents his age Bob was trying to separate himself from his parents and identify instead with his friends. The decisions Bob made were based primarily on information from his friends—who were generally just as confused as he was. They spent time together in school and out of school, and they were all trying to figure out how to fit into the groups at school and in the community: classes, teams, clubs, lunch table groups, and neighborhood groups. Bob spent much of his time with Frank and Ramon, discussing how to act and what to say. They were also trying to figure out girls. It was all very complicated.

Bob was not conscious of the variety of choices available to him. Issues were black or white, with very few options in between. When Bob liked something, he really liked it. When he disliked something, he truly hated it. For instance, Bob decided all he wanted was a pair of special high-topped sport shoes. Only one very expensive brand would satisfy him. Bob's parents were not ready to spend so much money on a pair of shoes, but Bob wasn't interested in anything else. The argument went on for several weeks, until a new computer game became the focus of Bob's desires. Finding middle ground was a difficult task for Bob.

Leadership Information

Bob unconsciously heard and saw much about leadership and leaders throughout his life. He compiled culturally accepted information, passed on through his family, community, school, and friends. This information told him who leaders are, how leaders are selected, and what leadership is. Watching his mother and father make big decisions about the family, he saw two people sharing leadership in this context. He had a teacher in school who let the class make choices about how they could do some assignments. There was also a soccer coach, when Bob was younger, who didn't allow any variation to his many rules; this was the kind of arbitrariness that Bob associated with a true leader. The traditional, autocratic leader was easy for Bob to identify; he didn't recognize the fact that his parents and his teacher were displaying other types of leadership.

Bob believed that to be a leader you had to be at the right spot at the right time, be from the right family, or have "all the qualities" that make people leaders. You had to have good looks, money, popularity, intelligence, and athletic ability. Bob couldn't see himself fitting this description at all. He was busy trying to be the same as all of his friends. "I know who leaders are," he said; "I see them on

TV. They dress good, speak good, and have a lot of money. They are famous and important." Bob thought leaders were impressive and far removed from himself. He identified the principal of his school and the captain of the boy's basketball team as leaders in his world. He found it very difficult to imagine himself taking charge of a situation. He thought leadership was something held by one member of a group, the "leader"; he couldn't see himself assuming that role. He had little insight into how to behave or perform as a leader in a group; he really had no notion that leadership abilities and opportunities were within his reach.

Bob spent most of his time in groups of friends. His leadership abilities and skills were being developed in these groups, yet he had little information about the workings of a group and the ways in which groups progress through stages. He didn't notice that each group he belonged to followed a predictable path. For Bob, everything that happened in his groups was unexpected, so he spent much of his time reacting to situations and therefore had no time to think or respond critically: no time to become aware of and try out his latent leadership skills. Because of his lack of information, he missed leadership learning opportunities. Bob was unable to take what he learned from one situation and apply it to another.

Leadership Attitude

Bob believed that leadership was something external; other people defined leadership, and other people possessed those abilities. His ideas were narrow, so that any attempt to explore his own leadership potential was difficult. He believed that leadership positions were prestigious and exclusive: there was a small, elite group of his peers who were chosen to be in charge. Bob thought that it was not for him to say he had leadership potential; he saw no choice in whether or not he would become a leader. It never occurred to him that he had leadership qualities within himself. For example, one of Bob's friends nominated him to be the homeroom representative for his class. Since he had just come to the high school from middle school, he didn't know most of the people in his homeroom. He felt shy and uncomfortable, so he quickly turned down the opportunity. Bob was flattered that one of his friends would nominate him, but he had no confidence that he would actually be elected, and no idea what to do if he were.

Bob's attitude about leadership revolved around issues of power and control. Since he was not in any formal or even informal leadership position, he believed that he had no power to lead and no control over decision-making processes. Leadership was beyond his reach. When he *was* offered a leadership opportunity, he didn't know what to do with it. His attitude was that he, in fact, *couldn't* do it: that he wasn't a leader.

Communication Skills

Bob's more advanced communication skills were just beginning to develop. Bob often experienced breakdowns in the communication cycle of sending, receiving, and responding to messages: some crucial part would be missed and the process would be interrupted. The problem was that Bob was more concerned with getting a message out than with making sure it was received.

He also had difficulty listening to others. Sometimes instead of listening he was busy rehearsing what he was going to say next; in other cases he was simply daydreaming or half-listening. This was a way for Bob to glide through conversations; many times he would pretend to listen on the phone to friends while a single complete message almost never got through. The phone was a big part of Bob's life. Girls were starting to call his house, and he was teased constantly by his little sisters; even his father would join in the ribbing. His mother just wanted to know what they wanted when they called. The girls usually only wanted to say hello, but sometimes they asked him to go to the ice garden to skate. He would go if Frank or Ramon was going, and if they could find someone to drive them. This was a good way to spend time with girls without being paired off with one of them in particular.

Bob almost always used *you* and *we* in his speech. His habit of speaking this way allowed him to avoid taking responsibility for his own ideas. It was very important to him that he not be perceived as different from the "guys." Using a collective pronoun gave him a sense of security, of safety in numbers. Using a pronoun that didn't single him out was safe because it relieved him of the stress of taking ownership of his views. Bob became very awkward and uncomfortable when he was asked to pay attention to this particular speech habit and attempt to use more personal statements. He would try but quickly return to his usual speech pattern.

Bob didn't know much about nonverbal communication in others, even though his own behavior often adjusted automatically in response to nonverbal signals from others. He was more focused on himself than those around him. For example, we asked Bob how he knew when his father was in a bad mood without being told so; he quickly responded that he knew from certain signals. He knew not to ask for anything when his dad slammed the front door in coming home from work. Bob was unaware that he gathered knowledge of nonverbal signals and used it to make behavior decisions, though he would do just that. The fact that he was unaware of this knowledge made it more difficult for him to apply the information to other people and other situations. This had nothing to do with Bob's intelligence; he was just beginning to put old and new information together.

Awareness of personal presence is an important aspect of being a leader, but Bob possessed very little appreciation of the effect that his personal presence had on others. He made poor eye contact with others and tended to orient his body away from the person he was speaking to. He couldn't figure out why people had difficulty understanding him. He wasn't aware that the messages he was sending were not being received with clarity. He didn't realize that although he might say one thing verbally, his body would send an entirely different message.

Decision-Making Skills

Bob did make some decisions every day. He decided whether or not to smoke cigarettes, drink alcohol, stay in school, or follow parental advice. He did not spend much time deliberating these decisions or thinking about their consequences. He also didn't consider the fact that how he made these choices was an indication of his leadership abilities. In fact he didn't often *have* many choices, so he had little experience making decisions. His life was for the most part structured and scheduled by parents and teachers.

Bob's decision making was often inconsistent; he said one thing and then did something else. This didn't seem at all unusual to him, because he didn't notice that there was a discrepancy between what he did and what he said. His values were in the formative stage. Once Bob told his mother that he would help his elderly next-door neighbor cut the grass. He always said he liked Mr. Blattner (not his real name), but right before he left to go next door and begin the chore Frank called to invite Bob to go to the local amusement park, and Bob said yes. He didn't even go and tell Mr. Blattner he was not going to cut the grass that day; instead, he hurried over to Frank's so that they could get a ride to the park. Bob did feel guilty, but he couldn't figure out any other choice that would have allowed him to do both things. The values that he claimed were important to him were not consistent with his behavior; pressure from his friends made it too difficult for him to stand apart from them. Conforming to the decisions of the group was typical behavior for Bob.

Bob's decision-making processes were also influenced by his perception of his chances of success and failure. If he believed he would be successful, then he was more encouraged to take the risk of making a decision to try something new; if he felt there was a good chance he would fail, then he did not even try. Bob had little confidence in his ability to be successful, so he abstained from making any decision at all until someone else made it for him.

Sometimes his decisions seemed impulsive and reactive, because his self-assessments were not always accurate. For instance, he was very confident that he would do well in a spelling contest when he was in the seventh grade, and when he misspelled a number of words he was surprised. This experience made him wary of taking part in academic competitions later on. Sometimes this tendency worked the other way around; he would make overly optimistic self-assessments, but so long as his evaluations of his own competence were not too far off the mark they would leave him feeling some confidence to try new things.

Stress-Management Skills

"My parents embarrass me; they talk too much." According to Bob, the primary sources of stress in his life were his parents, peers, siblings, money, and school. One of Bob's biggest stresses during his freshman year in high school was the report card for his second grading period. He grew tired of doing the work in his English class, so he stopped completing homework assignments altogether. He also stopped paying attention in class, and by the end of the grading period he faced having to get at least a B on the final test in order to bring his grade for the class up to a C. Because his mother was a teacher and felt strongly about his maintaining decent grades, Bob was certain she would hit the ceiling if he got a D for the class. Bob tried to study hard for the test, but since he had missed so much information he was totally lost. On report card day panic set in; during the long bus ride home he felt sick to his stomach, knowing there was nothing to do but face his parents with the D he had received.

Bob had little stress-management information. He only knew that certain things made him feel bad and that he wanted to avoid those situations. If he were to fully realize his potential, he would have to learn to be proactive, expand his limited repertoire of stress-management skills, and let go of his typically reactive way of managing stress. He didn't have strategies for lessening stress, because he didn't believe he had much control over it. Instead, he would react to it by oversleeping, eating too much junk food, and watching television endlessly. He talked back to his teachers, came to class late, and lied.

These were not particularly effective techniques to reduce stress; moreover, they had negative consequences. Bob rarely displayed more positive reactions to stress, which can create a drive that pushes a person to a higher level of performance. For some people, stress is an incentive to try harder to reach their goals. Bob did not view stress as positive and would frequently just shut down when faced with it. His ability to manage stress effectively would be critical in his leadership development. Without these skills, he had few means to buffer the stress involved in trying out new behaviors and skills.

Working with Stage One Adolescents

Bob is a typical adolescent: being a leader is not part of what he thinks about. When we look at adolescents in the awareness stage, we do find a small percentage who feel that they are leaders and who willingly seek out opportunities to take leadership positions. They usually define leadership as "being the boss, being in control, and telling people what to do." This is exactly how they try to lead, with varied results. When they are successful, they are usually praised and rewarded by adults. Adolescents in Stage One need to learn about different ways of being a leader so that they can begin to develop and use a range of leadership behaviors. For example, when we helped Bob think about the fact that his parents were both leaders in sharing the decision making for his family, he was able to see that more than one person at a time can act as a leader in a group. Bob's reflection about the teacher who offered the class choices in completing assignments provided him with still another model of leadership to consider.

Often when we select Stage One adolescents to participate in leadership activities, they think that we must have made a mistake.

They doubt their own abilities. They don't think of themselves as leaders, and this new viewpoint confuses them. They fear they will have to change their behavior and begin acting differently, and they are not comfortable with being unlike the rest of their friends. It's risky. Parents and teachers sometimes question our selection as well, which further validates adolescents' perception that they are not leaders. Adolescents don't think it's possible that they are being singled out for leadership development. After being assured that they are exactly the individuals we are seeking, they begin to look at themselves differently. They also begin to look at others differently, because they have never considered that adolescents exactly like themselves could have leadership potential. We take the first step in the leadership development process just by stopping and recognizing these adolescents as leaders.

In our work with Stage One adolescents, we make a distinction between the being and doing aspects of leadership, while also helping teens think about their own leadership styles. When working with adolescents, one finds it critical to differentiate from the start between transactional and transformational leadership. We recommend beginning by focusing on transformational leadership in particular. Teenagers know about transactional leadership, since in most cases this is how they have defined leadership throughout their whole lives. We want them to think differently about being a leader and about the process of leadership. The focus on transformational leadership provides a new viewpoint for them to consider. Over time, we can reach a balance between transformational and transactional leadership.

We have found that certain knowledge and skills are critical if Stage One adolescents are to understand and experience leadership in their everyday lives. Figure 4.1 shows which knowledge and skills are most beneficial when working with these adolescents. It is equally important to give them a structure that allows them to rehearse how to act as leaders in their own lives. Creating an environment where adolescents actively learn from experience through activities and discussions allows the focus to be on both

Figure 4.1 Stage One Focus Areas

	Transformational	Transactional
Leadership Information	Group expectations Group dynamics Group stages Experiential learning	Why and what of leadership development
Leadership Attitude	Awareness of personal leadership Being kind and fair to peers	Shared group leadership Assertiveness
Communication Skills	Distinctions made among aggressiveness, assertiveness, and passivity	Verbal and nonverbal messages
Decision-Making Skills	Awareness of decision making as a leadership quality Understanding of how the belief system affects decisions Shared decision making	Active awareness of the decision-making process Decision making to move the process
Stress-Management Skills	Identifying personal stress	Three levels of stress management

transformational and transactional leadership. Chapter Seven thoroughly discusses working with teenagers in groups, a methodology we have found to be quite effective in leadership development. However, ongoing efforts to recognize and support youth leadership development are also crucial in the larger community, in schools, and in families.

Leadership Information

Adolescents in Stage One need concrete leadership information that is connected to their lives. Since they live, play, and work in groups, we should spend time with them exploring how groups work and the roles of the adolescent as a member of a group. They need a road map for what to expect if they are to behave differently in the groups of their lives. Behaving differently might mean speaking up and venturing an opinion that contradicts what others have said, or, for an impulsive talker, just being quiet and listening. Adolescents can try out alternative actions if they have a safe atmosphere in which to do so.

Adolescents are interested in discovering how learning takes place as part of the group experience. But at first most of them aren't sure how this fits in with leadership. Through leadership education and opportunities, we can demonstrate how leaders learn by reflecting on their experiences. In particular, we focus on the crucial task of demystifying leadership and dispelling myths and stereotypes of leadership development.

Sometimes you wonder if this information about leadership is making any impression on an individual adolescent. Chances are that at times, especially in the beginning, it isn't. If the information isn't referred to again in future leadership education and opportunities, it is lost in the avalanche of input that the adolescent experiences. Early leadership information is best viewed as just a foundation to build on through repeated efforts.

Leadership Attitude

Another focus of our work with Stage One adolescents is to help them become aware of their ability to lead by placing value on each individual adolescent and his or her potential for leadership. We show them that leadership is not defined as a rigid, unbending set of tasks, structures, and responsibilities. Instead, we present it as a gathering of energy and creativity with a purpose; it is personal development that benefits the individual and the group, whether it is a family or a gathering of friends, classmates, coworkers, or neighbors. Leadership ability is a dimension of their own personality that adolescents can consider as they form their identity.

"I am a leader." Encourage Stage One adolescents to grapple

with their personal leadership potential and abilities. Try to give them realistic information, since leadership development is not central to their lives. Help them view it as a long-term investment: a strengthening and deepening of their repertoire of skills and abilities. Emphasize that kindness and fairness to their peers—and themselves—within groups is an important aspect of leadership. This translates into creating nonviolent and emotionally safe environments for self-exploration. The young person needs to learn how to foster self-respect and uphold certain standards of behavior. The transactional side of improving adolescent leadership attitudes focuses on encouraging and supporting shared group leadership. Show adolescents how to be assertive; let them know that it is okay to share their thoughts and opinions. Encourage them to see themselves as active members of their groups, individuals who contribute to the group's direction and energy.

Communication Skills

Stage One adolescents are only beginning to become aware of their effect on others. They are just starting to recognize when effective communication is taking place and when it isn't. Most teens have a great deal of difficulty with communication, but even so they are usually quite interested in learning more. Their communication hang-ups exist not only in their interactions with adults but in those with peers as well, so their desire to improve their skill in this area is often very strong. Disassembling the subject of communication and looking at its individual components can be a useful way to demonstrate how the cycle of communication typically malfunctions. Activities that help adolescents look first at themselves and then outward toward others are very effective in helping them learn about communication.

Most Stage One adolescents have not yet learned to be consciously aware of body language, and so this is an area that they are usually very willing to explore. Some adolescents may have been coached by their parents to stand up tall and look people in the eye when speaking to them, but these are actions usually taken to be a matter of politeness, not for the express purpose of improving communication. Most teens don't realize that a slumped body posture and poor eye contact confuse the message they are trying to send, thereby making communication more difficult and less effective.

Some cultures have different rules for different situations. Looking a person directly in the eye, for instance, is a sign of aggression in some cultures. Given the fact that societies differ in various respects, it is important for adults to know the communication styles that are appropriate for each culture, thus altering what constitutes good communication. As is the case when writing an essay, you must know your audience before you can deliver your information effectively.

Another communication difficulty that adolescents in this stage encounter is that they often don't listen actively; therefore the communication cycle is again interrupted. Not only do they fail to fully receive the message being conveyed to them but they are unable to respond to that message, which ends the conversation. Adolescents have a very well developed ability to tune out those speaking to them, whether it be on the phone, in the classroom, at home, or even with a friend. Good communication is virtually impossible when the participants don't actively listen. Spending time on this subject and connecting it with leadership helps the adolescent understand why he must be an active listener and an active questioner (clarifier) to be an effective leader.

Decision-Making Skills

Stage One adolescents show little consciousness of the variety of choices available to them in making a decision. They can clearly point out the extremes, but the options in between are left unexplored. They need help in learning how to gather information, study alternatives aside from the most obvious ones, and make good decisions based on careful thought.

Discovering what it is that these adolescents truly value is one way to begin exploring with them the area of decision making. We can also discuss with them the difference between values and attitudes. Values are strongly held beliefs that are unshakable. Attitudes are currently held beliefs that are more transient in nature. These are important distinctions, because a person's behavior is driven by his or her values and attitudes. An important question to ask Stage One adolescents is, "Does your behavior match your values?" Simply connecting these concepts helps them build an awareness of themselves that will play an important part in their leadership development.

Stress-Management Skills

Stress is a normal part of life. Since Stage One adolescents often continue to deny their leadership potential, we ask them to talk openly about the stress involved with the process of change: the risks, benefits, and opportunities involved in making changes in their lives. They sometimes resist any attempts to look at how they might be leaders. We try not to push them to identify the word *leader* with themselves, because doing so only causes more stress.

At this stage, the best thing we can do is often simply to help adolescents be aware of what stress feels like and identify some ways to cope. It is important for adolescents to identify the primary causes of stress in their lives and explore a small number of healthy ways to relieve that stress. Relaxation techniques can be very effective stress releasers. Relaxation exercises are usually met with giggles in the beginning, but after a few repetitions participants come to enjoy and benefit from the activity.

Reflections on Stage One: Preparation

Most adolescents (indeed, some adults) live their lives in Stage One of leadership development. They accept all the cultural and societal norms and traditions about who leaders are, how people become leaders, and what leaders do. Leadership is externalized from their being.

The primary task in Stage One is to recognize a young person's leadership potential and then prepare him to move to a higher level. Adolescents are very comfortable in Stage One. They tend to think that most teenagers can't do more or be more. Sometimes adolescents' life situations are too overwhelming to allow them to look at their leadership potential, but for most this is not the case. With the majority of adolescents, we can work successfully to prepare them to move to the next stage of development, helping them see themselves and be seen by others as active and conscious participants in their interactions in the family and among friends, teachers, neighbors, employers, and coworkers.

Chapter Five

Stage Two: Interaction

I am a leader. I have choices. I can do lots of
activities.

—*Katie, tenth grade*

Suddenly these phrases seem to fit. Teenagers in Stage Two of leadership development, the interaction stage, wrestle with the idea that they are leaders. Stage Two is about action. It's testing possibilities, reaching limits, resting, and reflecting.

Katie

Katie was an energetic fourteen-year-old when we first met her in a meeting at the local Boys and Girls Club. She had become a member of the club about six months before and was happy to be part of a large group, which included two of her best friends who lived down the street from her. Katie also had a small group of girlfriends with whom she spent time at school. She had one older sister, Carlyn, and they both lived with their mother in a small house in the city. Their mother and father divorced three years earlier; their father lived in another state. They got to see him only infrequently, which Katie didn't like very much.

Katie was quiet and reserved around adults. Her grades in school were just a little above average. At the time we met, in a leadership workshop, Katie was very much in Stage One of leadership development. Like Bob (in Chapter Four), she believed that leadership was something reserved for adults and a few select young people, but certainly not for herself. Katie was uncomfortable taking risks—

venturing outside her tight circle of friends was to her a risk, for instance—but she was beginning to try out new experiences of this sort by joining the Boys and Girls Club and by participating in the leadership workshop we invited her to. Also like Bob, she had a difficult time using the word *I* rather than *we*. She was compliant when asked to do something but volunteered infrequently. Katie didn't see herself as a leader.

As she progressed through the tenth grade in school, we noticed some changes in her behavior patterns. She joined the girl's softball team, and her circle of friends began to expand. This was new behavior not only because the activity was new but because she joined the team without any of her close friends doing so along with her. Carlyn had played softball with the team when she was Katie's age, and she encouraged Katie to join too. Katie's mother was pleased that she was making new friends and doing something athletic. The team was made up of girls from many different areas of the school district. During practice and while traveling to the away games, she became increasingly comfortable with the new group. Her comfort allowed her to practice many of the skills she had learned in the leadership workshop at the Boys and Girls Club the previous summer. What particularly helped was the information she received about communication. She learned how important it was to listen to others and try to understand another person's point of view. Katie knew she didn't have to agree with everyone, but it could still be important and interesting to listen to them.

Katie began to think that maybe she *could* be a leader—not all of the time, but sometimes. She realized there were situations and activities in which she actually influenced people's decisions, and where being assertive by stating her opinions contributed to completion of a project. The concept of transformational leadership was definitely growing in her. She was becoming aware that she could remain herself and still be a leader, despite not seeing herself as tremendously outgoing or popular.

Katie considered trying out for the school play and joining a new club after school. She was becoming more aware of how much she was learning. She began to ask more questions about the things that interested her. The idea of performing in the school play was terrifying but intriguing. She stayed after school the first day of play tryouts. As she walked into the auditorium, she held her breath. But when she saw that there were only seven other people trying out for the ten parts, she realized that it wouldn't be so hard after all. The drama teacher was very helpful and promised to work with all of the students to pull the play together. She worked on her small part every day after school, and by the time opening night arrived she was confident that all would go well. The play was a big success. Katie had made new friends and experienced a team working well together. She was sad when it was all over; she recognized that the group experience was at an end.

When Katie talked about being a leader, she spoke of both a sense of adventure and feelings of anxiety. Some of her friends understood what she meant, while others thought the whole idea of leadership was stupid. Katie was able to talk about accepting her nervousness as her awareness of her leadership ability strengthened. She was very interested in practicing her leadership abilities in different settings and building a repertoire of skills to influence others. She often wondered why all of her friends didn't share her enthusiasm about doing different things. Once she thought it would be great if all her friends went together to serve Thanksgiving dinner at a soup kitchen. Not one of her friends wanted to go. This was very upsetting for Katie, but she talked her mother and sister into joining her. They had a very satisfying experience that Thanksgiving.

Katie became much more willing to volunteer on her own, felt more competent interacting with others, grew more willing to try new things, had more courage than before, began taking more risks, and was becoming more open-minded. She was taking the first steps toward becoming a unique individual and being much more aware of things that were going on around her.

Although Katie was gaining awareness of herself and her world, she didn't know everything; she just sometimes thought she did. The bits of knowledge she had were often enough to encourage her to take some risks. However, her enthusiasm often dampened when reality turned out not to match what she had imagined it to be. Katie plunged into projects without much thought about the process required to accomplish them. She and her friends decided that it would be fun to have music playing during lunch at school. The idea sounded great, and Katie even got the principal to agree to buy a few new speakers for the cafeteria. However, the eventual downfall of the project was the inability of the student body to agree on what type of music should be played. Katie hadn't thought ahead about a method for peacefully selecting the music, so there was trouble whenever music was played. The school decided to end the experiment as a result of the strife.

Leadership Information

Katie began to use what she was learning about leadership and leaders. She took the information she gained in Stage One and solidified it through her experiences and interactions with people. She was becoming more aware of differences among leaders. For example, she was aware of how leaders approach problems and of various styles of interaction. She understood the difference between doing leadership tasks and being a leader. Katie was most concerned with doing leadership tasks, since this is the type of behavior that is usually rewarded at school and at home. At the same time, she had a growing sense that to truly influence people she had to *be* a leader, or "walk the talk." She was still a little mixed up about the concepts of transformational and transactional leadership, but she no longer thought that a leader needed to be a "great person" or be in the right place at the right time.

Katie had information about her leadership abilities and skills and about how she performed as a leader in groups at school, in the community, and at home. She had some awareness of what it meant to learn from experience, and she began to use experiential learning tools. All of the activities in which she participated provided her with more information about herself and others. She was beginning to understand interactions between people in groups. As she become more aware of group dynamics and group development, she was able to use this information to promote her own experiential learning.

Even though she often understood interactions between people, she was seldom able to intervene in any way. On many occasions, she asked adults or friends to help her reflect on something she had just experienced. She was usually able to see patterns of behavior in herself and others, though, and tried to figure out how to use that information.

Leadership Attitude

Katie could be assertive at times. She contributed to discussions, and she helped make decisions in activities with friends and during collaborative school projects. Her definition of leadership greatly expanded, and as a result her attitude toward herself and her friends changed. She could see situations where she demonstrated her leadership ability, and she recognized opportunities to lead when they arose in many different settings. Katie began to realize that leadership can look different from one situation to another. During one leadership session, she acknowledged that her leadership abilities didn't mean speaking loudly and getting what she wanted all of the time. Her attitude was that leadership was both attainable and desirable. She began to see that leadership skills could help her get along better with others.

Once Katie recognized that she possessed leadership abilities, she was much less concerned with getting power and control and more focused on how the group process worked. Katie strove to include others in activities. This was often a difficult task because they were not always cooperative, and Katie would be left to do the job herself or give it up. She learned about cultural diversity and about individual differences among her friends. However, she was not always able to accept differences of opinion. In her enthusiasm, she often believed that everyone should think the same way she did. When she became a student helper at the Boys and Girls Club leadership workshop for younger teens the summer following her sophomore year, she often expressed frustration about workshop participants, citing their lack of focus and their resistance to new ideas about leadership. It was difficult for her to accept that not everyone thought the same way she did. Katie had an oversimplified view of the ease with which she could accomplish tasks. She never planned for the setbacks that would inevitably block her path. She was always overly optimistic. When problems arose, they caused her stress; patience was not her strong suit.

Communication Skills

Katie was interested in knowing how to convey her message to others. She wanted to know how to disagree with a teacher or parent and yet enjoy a positive outcome. Katie felt as if her words were often misunderstood; this impression motivated her to concentrate on expressing herself more clearly. She worked on stating her desires with greater clarity, but she still often missed a fundamental part of communication: listening. This was her greatest difficulty with communication. Listening required Katie to consider the ideas of the person she was talking to, while keeping in mind that their opinions might have value and could influence her own ideas.

Katie began to make distinctions between different ways to communicate. She enjoyed figuring out how to best get what she wanted, and she took more risks to achieve her goals. Being assertive was still a new and largely unfamiliar concept. Katie knew that being assertive meant that she had the right to her own feelings, beliefs, and opinions, while recognizing that others have their rights as well. Katie was gaining her voice as an individual and a leader.

Decision-Making Skills

Katie was excited about the choices available to her. She some-times sought advice regarding a particular decision, but she also made many decisions on her own. Katie even started to think about her future, and began taking advantage of opportunities when they came along. On one occasion, she was asked to be part of a group that served as an advisory board for her high school prin-cipal. It felt worthwhile to be a part of the group, because she saw that others listened to her ideas and valued her input. She realized that some things at school really did change as a result of her involvement, while others did not: "I understand a little more about how decisions are made."

Katie was starting to understand that adults were not the soli-tary source of power and control when it came to making decisions in her life. Instead, she learned that she was capable of making decisions herself. She sometimes encountered more difficulty with adults as a result of her increased confidence in questioning adult points of view; her forthrightness caused tension for herself and adults alike. However, she could also be quite vulnerable to self-doubt and often had second thoughts about her abilities. She retreated from disagreements while denying her anxiety and ten-sion. In the past, her mother had taken responsibility for most of her daughter's decisions, so the process of decision making was both frightening and exciting for Katie. She began to think that she alone knew what was best for herself and sometimes defiantly objected to her mother's opinions. Most of the time the situation worked out fine, but sometimes the two had to agree to disagree.

Katie's decision making became more deliberate. She grew bet-ter able to consider her options and the possible consequences of her actions before she made a decision. One time, Katie wanted to spend the weekend camping with a friend's family. The only prob-lem was that she had a final exam on Monday morning. She weighed her choices and thought about the consequences of each, not without some anxiety. She then decided not to go, because she wouldn't have enough time to study for her test. She was able to think ahead and consider consequences in the near future.

She began to better understand the consequences of her decisions, both negative and positive. This was true especially for decisions about something she was good at. In an area of competence, where Katie felt sure of herself, it was easier for her to decide responsibly and thoughtfully. However, decision making was generally a struggle for her because she was torn between her need to belong to the group—and therefore do what the group did—and her growing sense of competence and need to pursue her own interests, which often differed from those of her friends.

As Katie made more decisions, she gained greater insight into the cause and effect of her choices; ultimately she formed a more internal locus of control. She realized that she could determine the outcome of many situations.

Stress-Management Skills

The natural consequence of Katie's becoming involved was over-involvement. When she got her first taste of empowerment, she wanted to do everything and join everything. Prioritizing was not a skill she used widely, and she soon found herself overextended and overwhelmed. She didn't recognize her overinvolvement until it cut into her sleep, resulting in increased difficulty getting up; cut into her studies, resulting in lower grades; and affected her health, causing her to get sick more frequently.

Katie felt as if she could do it all as she entered her junior year of high school. She maintained a good grade average and was active in many groups, including the school newspaper, the softball team, and the Leadership Club. She got a job at Burger Haven, a fast-food restaurant, and still continued to participate in all of the activities she had previously enjoyed. She soon began to feel pressed for time, and because of the constraints of her schedule she found herself eating many of her meals at the restaurant. She gained ten pounds and was constantly tired. She didn't feel that she had time to be a part of activities she used to enjoy. This went on for six weeks, until she finally made a decision to cut her hours at work. It made a big difference. She decided that a smaller paycheck was worth the increase in free time. By figuring out a way to keep her job and still do the things she enjoyed, she learned that she had the power to make changes in her life.

Katie needed help to manage stress. Her self-defeating behavior, which stemmed largely from the stress of trying new roles, tended to manifest itself in an attitude that the work was just too hard and that she couldn't do it after all; maybe she really couldn't be a leader. Her ability to manage this stress productively was important to her continued development as a leader.

Working with Stage Two Adolescents

"They want to do everything; they have big ideas, but don't know how to put them into action. They make lots of assumptions about what others think and believe. They always underestimate how long something will take." These remarks are common among adults who work with Stage Two adolescents. Working with adolescents in this stage requires knowledge of how they think and what they still need to learn about their own leadership abilities. Adolescents at this stage are eager to learn more about leadership. They have information and experiences that have helped them improve their interactions in groups. Their view of the world is broadening, and new leadership experiences help them become more skillful as leaders.

One misconception that many adults have about adolescents in Stage Two is that these teens can now work independently of adults, producing wonderful projects that are exactly what the adults had in mind. This is not the case. Many adults are disappointed to find that these adolescents may actually not be effective at producing a product or completing a task because they are abundantly eager to be involved but don't have the foggiest notion of what to do once the task is in front of them. Adolescents in Stage Two are not fully prepared to work on their own. They continue to need support and guidance. In particular, adults can help focus adolescents' attention on group dynamics among their peers during classes and activities. Adults, especially parents, play a major role in helping adolescents set priorities and manage stress. Older siblings and peers frequently provide positive role models as well.

Without this support, adolescents are at risk of having their leadership development derailed: they question the importance of leadership development and are not quite sure how leadership fits into their lives. Support from adults validates the mix of feelings and anxiety adolescents experience as they develop their leadership potential. It connects teenagers to the larger group, whether their family, school, or community, thereby providing them with a context for understanding their development in relation to others (peers, family, teachers, and so on). The danger for adolescents in Stage Two is that they question their own abilities to the point that they do not believe they are leaders. When these doubts arise, they may regress to Stage One beliefs and behaviors.

We could see the importance of such support as Katie moved to expand her activities and circle of friends. Since most adolescents in the early stages of leadership development define leadership very narrowly, they do not include themselves in the definition. Teenagers like Katie usually have a very tight circle of friends with whom they feel comfortable. Katie was originally content to have two girlfriends make up her entire social circle. By starting to make the transition to Stage Two and entering new groups without the help of her two close friends, she was showing a new independence and confidence. Joining the softball team was her first adventure without her best friends. Because Carlyn played softball before her, it was easier for her to see herself on the team. Her sister had liked it and her mother was encouraging, so she thought it just might work—and it did. Because Katie was successful in entering the new group, she felt much more willing to try again in other situations.

This type of success is a powerful force for adolescents and helps them go on to take more risks.

In the second stage of leadership development, Katie was eager to be involved in more activities and sometimes even took on leadership roles. She demonstrated transactional leadership when she asked her friends to come and help at the soup kitchen during her junior year in high school. When her friends didn't want to join her, she was disappointed. She was motivated to *do* something (transactionally) for others, and she couldn't understand why her friends didn't want to do the same thing.

Katie wasn't always successful in the projects she undertook. She had lots of energy but little direction, and she was not yet able to work independently with consistent success. Katie still needed structure and support from the adults in her life. Regular meeting times and activities that support continued leadership development are helpful for Stage Two adolescents. Their ability to use their leadership skills is enhanced by continued guidance and support through activities directed by adults. At the same time, it is helpful to remember that activities and group meetings with Stage Two teens do not necessarily proceed as predicted. Expect spurts of progress and apparent relapses; this is all part of the normal process of leadership development for Stage Two youth. New insights come up along the way, and their course of development adjusts to accommodate changes in their way of thinking. It is imperative to have a plan in place at the start—but wise to evaluate and adjust the plan as the adolescents progress.

With Stage Two adolescents, we want to focus on supporting the teens' actions and developing their capacity to fully use their leadership abilities. A balanced approach between transformational and transactional leadership remains important. It's typical for adolescents to overload themselves with doing leadership (as opposed to being a leader). They take naturally to the more active sorts of leadership. Activity, however, should not be confused with development and progress. Being an autocratic leader in one activity (or five activities) only fortifies old stereotypes and stymies progress and development. In fact, in these situations adolescents are at risk of becoming overwhelmed and regressing to the Stage One beliefs that they are not leaders and don't have leadership abilities. It is therefore important to focus on *both* aspects of leadership development, doing leadership and being a leader. Together, they help teenagers to keep their balance and perspective.

Working with Stage Two youths differs from working with those in Stage One in that the former have awareness of their ability and potential to be leaders. Developmentally, these adolescents are more advanced, although they may not know what to do with their talents as yet. They are vulnerable to anxiety and insecurity concerning their abilities. As mentioned earlier, support from adults and peers is critical at this stage. The specific foci in terms of information and skills in Stage Two are illustrated in Figure 5.1.

Leadership Information

Adolescents in Stage Two begin to use the information they have gathered about leadership. The concepts of experiential learning, group dynamics, and the stages of a group start to make sense and become useful tools. These are all transformational concepts, and they are needed before any emphasis is placed on transactional leadership skills. We must continuously reinforce leadership information from Stage One so that Stage Two adolescents can make the necessary connections between experience and application.

The transactional leadership information that is important in this stage is knowledge of systems, that is, learning how things work. *Who, where, when,* and *how* are helpful questions in learning about systems. Who do you need to talk to so as to get things done? Is it the principal, a director, a parent, or the mayor? If a group is working on a project, who has the power to say yes and help make it happen? Where do you find these yes-people, and when is the best time to do it? Then how do you go about requesting help? Adolescents in Stage Two don't automatically know the answers to

Figure 5.1 Stage Two Focus Areas

	Transformational	*Transactional*
Leadership Information	Internalizing • Group expectations • Group dynamics • Group stages • Experiential learning	Learning about a specific system (school or job) Learning to assess needs of self and others Developing and implementing realistic plans
Leadership Attitude	Validating attitudes Stabilizing attitudes Being ethical Being sensitive to others	Acting ethically and sensitively Referring to groups Referring to individuals
Communication Skills	Listening	Practicing assertiveness
Decision-Making Skills	Beginning to see all of the alternatives and consequences when making decisions	Practicing using a decision-making model
Stress-Management Skills	Managing the environment Changing perceptions of stressors Managing the self	Keeping a schedule Trying out new ways to cope Knowing when it's time to say no

all of these questions. They need to learn how to do the necessary tasks in being a leader.

Leadership Attitude

Stage Two adolescents most often have the attitude that they possess leadership abilities. They need constant support and encouragement to be sensitive to others and aware of their influence on others. It is an enthusiastic and sometimes overly optimistic attitude. They don't understand how things work, how long things take, or how realistic a project is. They are ready to conquer the world, and they believe that everyone else should feel the same way. This causes them problems in encountering disappointment when things don't go their way. Adults need to understand that disappointment is a natural part of this stage of leadership development, and that they can help adolescents regroup and learn from failures by reflecting on their experience.

Sensitivity to others can be developed by working in a group that has built a foundation of trust, so that all members are able to talk openly about how they are affected by the behavior of others. An example of this is conducting a reflective discussion at the end of a project, to answer such questions as "Who was instrumental in completing the project successfully?" "What skills did each member contribute in executing the project?" This exercise helps young people form clearer ideas about how they affected others.

Diversity training is an appropriate and beneficial booster session in Stage Two. Giving adolescents more information about different cultures, genders, religions, and races helps them form attitudes that are more receptive of all people, not just those in their circle of friends. Bringing together groups from different parts of the city is one way to accomplish this task with little difficulty, and it is very helpful in giving youth a sense of the bigger world.

It is also important for Stage Two adolescents to learn how to use groups and individuals as references. Most adolescents have resources around them that they don't even know exist: a research assistant in the local library who can help look up guides to writing resumes, or a health clinic counselor who has information on AIDS to be used in an English essay assignment. Being able to use people and groups as resources helps widen the world of adolescents, allowing them to access alternative sources of information. Adults show teens how to do this by first doing so themselves and pointing it out to young people, and then becoming the resource person who connects adolescents to other resources. "Running interference" for teens helps them avoid becoming discouraged when someone doesn't call them back about a project that is important to them. It also helps cut some of the red tape that teens encounter when they begin to explore the world outside their own.

Communication Skills

Listening is probably the most important communication skill that Stage Two adolescents should practice. Adults can continuously support a fuller understanding of communication by including activities that demonstrate the need to actively listen in order to be a leader. A leader must listen to all people, regardless of age or authority, to best understand what each person has to offer. Adults can provide opportunities for Stage Two adolescents to visit other environments, such as nursing homes and elementary schools, *just to listen*. This activity should be followed by a time of reflection so that the adolescents can share what they learned from people who are different from themselves.

Stage Two adolescents also need to practice being assertive. Assertiveness is the type of behavior that most often gets individuals what they want. However, we should also stress that this is not always the case; there are certain times when being passive (or aggressive) is the best course to follow. Assertiveness involves being able to directly state what you want and at the same time listen to the response of the other person. Here again, listening is a key component in effective communication.

Decision-Making Skills

When Stage Two adolescents make a decision, they become increasingly aware of the variety of choices possible in any given situation. This is a real difference from Stage One, where young people are conscious only of extremes and give little thought to consequences. Stage Two teens are open to ideas that may aid in finding the right alternative when making a decision. When focusing on the decision-making process, it is helpful to supply a simple framework for decision making. There are many good decision-making models that can help adolescents think about the components involved in making conscientious decisions. Figure 5.2 is a simple version of one such model.

This framework helps adolescents separate the parts of making a decision or solving a problem and become more aware of their responsibility in the decision-making process.

Stress-Management Skills

Managing stress in Stage Two is about finding a balance between all the things one *wants* to do and those one actually *can* do. Over-involvement brings on anxiety and frustration. In Stage One, adolescents need to identify sources of stress; in Stage Two they need to become more aware of healthy ways to cope with stress. When working with a group of youths in this stage, it is informative to hear what each one does when she becomes stressed. This discussion allows everyone to get some idea of the wide range of coping methods others find effective.

Developing a workshop on scheduling and planning can help youths find ways to effectively control the amount and type of activities to which they commit themselves. This is one way to visually demonstrate for adolescents the importance of keeping track of everything they do and managing their time more effectively.

Figure 5.2 Problem-Solving Model

Decision Making: A Problem-Solving Model

- Identify the decision or problem
- Research all of the alternatives
- Identify the consequences of the alternatives
- Choose the alternative that suits your values
- Evaluate the decision

Teaching these adolescents how to say no when they need to is worthwhile as well. Saying no to doing too much, or to doing something that is in conflict with their value system, is a continuing process for young people. Adolescents in Stage Two tend to be so excited about doing things that it is difficult for them to be selective. They need to become more aware of how their personal values can help regulate the types of activities they pursue.

This is a wonderful time for adults to work with adolescents, but caution should be exercised. Just when you think that teens are quite capable of doing what they set out to do, you discover they aren't. They still need adult support—even when they say they don't want it.

Reflections on Stage Two: Middle Stage

Stage Two is about support and balance. Adolescents in this stage are in the middle of the leadership development process. At times they regress to Stage One attitudes and behaviors. At other times, they stretch themselves to Stage Three and then relax back to Stage Two. Young people in Stage Two can become heavily involved in leadership activities; they often overextend and overcommit themselves. Keeping a balance between doing leadership tasks and being a leader is a constant struggle for these youths. Learning how to develop and maintain the support they need and establish this balance is a primary task for Stage Two adolescents. If the support and balance are in place and adolescents have a sense of themselves—"who I am, what I have, and what I can do"—they own the tools they need to allow them to move toward Stage Three. If the support and balance are not present, adolescents fall back to doubting that they are leaders. They derail their leadership development, perhaps never to develop it to its full potential.

Chapter Six

Stage Three: Mastery

I'm going to step up and do it.

—*Damian, twelfth grade*

Stage Three is about focused effort in small areas of one's life. For adolescents, it means using leadership skills and abilities to create and generate new interest and energy in some part of their lives. Stage Three involves having the energy, resources, and guidance to pursue a personal vision.

Damian

"I'd rather be sleepin' late and hangin' with my friends," Damian admitted.

It was a day in June when we were starting a new leadership workshop at Lewiston High School. Fifteen-year-old Damian came in the door looking sleepy and less than happy to be there. Two of his friends were with him, so he really didn't have to make an effort to be friendly to anyone else in the workshop. In September, Damian would begin the tenth grade at a large inner-city school. He lived with his mother and older brother in an apartment in the city. His mother pressured him to participate in the workshop, because leadership development could be useful and, she said, it was an honor that he was asked in the first place. Damian didn't quite agree. He had other things he'd rather do with his time, and besides, he wasn't a leader in school. He didn't do anything special there; he just showed up, hung out, and left. He didn't even always do his homework, and he didn't particularly like most of his teachers.

Despite this attitude, Damian participated in the workshop activities and even seemed to enjoy himself. He liked the lunches. He ate a lot of food. Hanging out during lunch was the highlight of his week. By the end of the week he was even talking to other participants he hadn't known before the weeklong workshop began. Damian didn't offer his opinions much in the large group setting, but he did have a voice in his small group; he shared his thoughts and helped the group make decisions. He talked about how much he appreciated his brother's teaching him to play basketball. His brother was a good basketball player and was also a student at a local community college. Their father had died when Damian was little, so his older brother was a father figure to him.

Damian finished the weeklong workshop by writing himself a letter, stating his goals for the upcoming school year. This final workshop assignment would be mailed to the authors of their own letters in October to act as a reminder of their participation in the leadership experience. Damian wrote honestly about what he learned during the leadership experience; he was very positive about the workshop and liked what it taught him. But during the carefree summer months, his memory faded considerably. By October, he was back to going along the way he always had.

He was comfortable with his three best friends and hadn't made an effort to get to know any new people at the start of the school year. One day, he came home and noticed his name on an envelope in the mail. The writing looked familiar. He realized when he opened it that it was the letter he had written to himself in June at the end of his leadership workshop. The letter talked about how cool it was to get to know new people and how good it felt to speak up in the group. He felt as though people listened to him, it said, and even respected him when he disagreed with other people in the group.

The letter came at a good time, just as Damian was trying to figure out if he should volunteer for a community service project in school. At first he thought that it might be a neat thing to do, but he couldn't talk any of his friends into going with him. They all said that they didn't want to give up their Saturday mornings to go to a nursing home to walk around and talk to residents. What would they say to them? Damian was on the verge of being talked out of joining when he received his letter. Moreover, he knew one girl who was going for sure, so he decided to go—at least this once. He was shocked on arrival at the nursing home to see the many residents sitting at the front door. Some of them were in wheelchairs, and some were just wandering around. Damian was introduced to Betsy; she was eighty-three years old and was delighted to have Damian talk with her. Actually, Betsy did most of the talking that day. She told him about what it was like growing up on a farm in Georgia.

When his group sat down later to talk about their experience at the nursing home (as part of the reflection process), the group facilitator asked, "What kind of leader do you feel you are?" Damian thought for a minute and then spoke. "I feel like I am the kind of leader that can listen. On Saturday, I met Betsy and she talked to me about what it was like seventy years ago on a farm." He went on to talk about how he felt needed, and how he felt that others listened to him as well. One of his biggest surprises was that he was able to have a good time without his close friends. He thought he might visit the nursing home again.

He did go back, and Betsy asked him what he was going to do after high school. He told her that he really didn't know, but that he wasn't sure college was for him. He felt able to try out ideas and thoughts with her; she took him seriously. He found subsequent visits to the nursing home encouraging; he didn't say anything to his close friends, but he began to think he could do more activities. He wasn't sure what doing more meant, but he did sign up to help with the winter food drive through his school, and he decided to try out for the basketball team. He was far from being a great player, but his attitude and skills were good. He thought he might actually be able to make it. And he did. Suddenly his schedule was very full.

By January, he was too busy to make it to the nursing home to visit Betsy. He had basketball practice after school every day, and there were often games in the evenings. He worked ten hours a week at an ice cream shop. His stress level rose, and he had few skills to cope with its consequences. What Damian did was ask for help. He talked to his brother, who at the time was himself balancing an almost full-time job while attending community college. Damian decided to stay committed to all the activities on his schedule, but he would make some changes in the future. For instance, he decided not to play basketball with the high school team after that season, instead just playing with his buddies for fun and relaxation.

During the summer between his sophomore and junior years Damian joined a work program. It turned out to be a chance for him to learn more about being an adult through his interaction with younger kids and the people he worked with, especially a man named Reggie. Reggie was really good with little kids; he was patient and was able to have fun playing basketball. He was thirty and liked to spend time talking to the young people who worked for the summer program. Damian and Reggie had long discussions about what was important in life and how good Damian was with the younger kids. By the end of the summer, he was in charge of his own small group of nine-year-old boys. They all thought Damian was so cool. He was having a great time.

Damian's junior year was busy. Reggie asked him to help out at the community agency that ran the summer program. Damian worked for the agency after school on three weekdays, and one day on the weekend. He tutored younger kids, played basketball, watched TV with them, and made their afternoon snacks (hot dogs, pizza, and juice) at the agency. He was paid for his time, and he used the money to buy clothes, shoes, and a beeper. If he went riding with a friend who had a car, he could help out with gas. But he spent most of the time with his friends, walking around, going to the gym to work out, playing video games, and watching television. Occasionally they would get a chance to drive around and hang out at different spots.

He decided to join the basketball team again in his junior year. The coach talked to his mother about the fact that Damian might be able to get a scholarship for college if he played and still did okay in school. Damian wasn't very enthusiastic, but he agreed to try to keep his grades up at school. This was difficult for him, because he felt that he was always behind. He would usually start out poorly, with D's and C's, and then fight to bring the grades up. By the end of the school year he didn't make honor roll, but he didn't get any D's or F's either.

Like Katie in Chapter Five, Damian was grappling with who he was and where this thing called leadership fit in to his life—if it fit in at all. By the time Damian was a senior in high school, he knew that for him leadership wasn't like being president of student council or captain of the basketball team; it was more personal. "I'm not 'doing leadership,'" he said; "I'm working on 'being a leader' in my family and with my friends." We saw this struggle in Damian, and we also saw many areas of success and positive change in his life. He was starting to widen his circle of friends; he recognized that being overcommitted caused him stress; he was becoming more skilled at talking and listening, not only with adults, but also with his peers; he was increasingly aware of his own leadership abilities; and along with being willing to keep in touch with Betsy he realized that he also got much from his visits to her. Damian didn't always keep things together. As basketball season progressed during twelfth grade, his grades dropped and he struggled with his commitment to the basketball team. He felt pressure from his friends, mother, and coach. By the end of the season, he was tired of school. At that point, he began to think about what it was he really liked to do. He concluded that what he really enjoyed was working with the children at the community agency.

Damian talked with Reggie at the community agency about the possibility of working at the agency again during the summer, and the next year when he was out of school. Damian didn't feel ready to go to college. His mother and brother had at one time encouraged him to think about college, but now they let the subject rest. He knew some people who were going to college, but he wasn't interested in going yet. One or two friends decided to join the army, and a lot of other kids he knew were just going to try to find a job to make money. Still others didn't know yet what they were going to do. Damian decided he really wanted to pursue the idea of working with kids in the community agency, or if not there then at some other agency that worked with kids. His pursuit of this goal of working with young children after high school and his ultimate success was quite a step up for Damian.

Leadership Information

Damian needed specific information that would help him make a decision. He had to figure out what would be helpful, and what might be too much for him. He wasn't comfortable going to the library to look at books about working with kids. He decided to talk with a full-time employee at the community agency about how he got his job. He also talked to the agency's van driver. He thought that maybe one day he would get a driver's license and could work as a driver. He asked Reggie about other people who might be able to give him information on working with kids. Reggie gave him the name of a supervisor in the city's recreational program. Damian also talked with his basketball coach and his brother about other possible jobs working with kids. Damian saw that all of these people could be sources of information. He felt encouraged that people were willing to talk with him, and others got to know about his interests. He was invited to help out at a couple of different events; one was sponsored by the city, another was sponsored by a community agency in a different part of the city. At both events, he got to meet some new people and he talked with them about programs and opportunities to work with young kids.

Leadership Attitude

Damian felt competent. His attitude was that he could achieve his vision for himself: "It doesn't have to be anything huge . . . I can do something." Damian was realistic about his strengths and weak-

nesses. This didn't mean that he suddenly stopped taking on too many activities and no longer felt overwhelmed; he still did so at times, but for the most part he was focused. He was no longer easily sidetracked.

Damian's attitude toward other people was also an important part of his changing views of leadership. He saw others as valuable sources of feedback. His friends, his mother, coworkers, Reggie, the basketball coach, his brother, and even a few teachers were role models. He looked at what they did and then evaluated what would be best for him; he didn't just do as they did but rather related their behavior and beliefs to his own life and adjusted his actions according to what made the most sense for him. He felt he could talk to people if he had questions about their actions and behavior.

He had a growing sense of what he thought was important, and he acted according to those values. He knew he was responsible for his own behavior. He tried to keep in mind that he wanted a balance between doing (transactional) and being (transformational) in his life. He liked being known as someone who could get things done. It made him feel good.

Communication Skills

Damian managed to keep up his visits with Betsy throughout his high school career, with only a few breaks when his schedule was too full. Each time, he learned more about the value of listening. Sometimes he didn't say much during the visits; nevertheless, he got a lot out of them. He was open to what Betsy had to say, even if it didn't always make much sense to him. With Betsy, he felt like a very competent listener and communicator. He asked her questions and learned much; his listening involved being sensitive to Betsy and the situation she was in.

Damian sometimes felt pressure to display transactional leadership skills: to be able to do such things as lead a meeting, speak in public, write well, use parliamentary procedure, and motivate a

group. Through his work at the community agency, he became a leader in the community. He was invited to be part of community youth panels and youth speak-out days. Damian also had an interest in writing, but he had to work very hard to express himself through written words. He even wrote a letter to the editor of the local newspaper the summer after he graduated from high school, and it was published. He was encouraged by this experience to write more.

Decision-Making Skills

Damian's decision to work with children was just the beginning of what turned out to be a long series of small decisions. Damian talked to a lot of people. He needed help considering his alternatives and the possible consequences of those alternatives. At times he was bogged down in the details and anxious, distracted, and sidetracked. During those periods he became frustrated and angry.

When an opportunity came up to work with the city parks department, he felt panicked to some extent. But he was also excited, and scared. He liked working with Reggie at the community agency but was interested in working in different parts of the city. Through a city basketball league, he had gotten to know people from all over the city. He liked being known around town. The city parks department job was sports-related, but this was not its only focus. It involved environmental education as well. He didn't know much about that field; in school he had done poorly in science and was now nervous about having to "catch up" again. He knew how that felt and didn't like it. At the same time, he saw the position as an opportunity to work with young children in a way he hadn't even imagined. He decided to take the position.

Stress-Management Skills

Damian had a lot of stress in his life. Stepping forward to pursue his interest meant that he was visible. People knew he was looking to

do something good and different. He didn't want to just hang out with his buddies all day watching TV, going to the gym, or playing ball. He still did a lot with his friends, but he wanted more.

He worked to change his perspective on things that caused him stress. He accepted that he was likely to be nervous about certain events and activities. Damian started to understand that things often happen over which he has no control. Originally, he would stew over everything that didn't go exactly the way he hoped. He recalled the difficulty in getting a group of teens excited about a holiday visit to the nursing home; he felt angry and bewildered when they didn't want to go. For a while, that setback discouraged Damian from pursuing more projects with groups.

After experiencing several such failures, he began learning to reevaluate the event (the stressor) and see the positive instead of the negative. This does not mean he no longer had feelings of pain, embarrassment, or anger. But he accepted that events do not always proceed as planned, and he became more open to the idea that he could learn from the experience no matter what its result. Once he understood this, he was able to rebuild and refocus his energy. Giving up control left him free to enjoy activities and learn from them. For example, he went with the city league to play in a basketball tournament in Chicago. He had never been to far-away Chicago before, and he was excited about going and trying to play the best he could. His team didn't win any trophies, but Damian still had fun. He particularly enjoyed being with the coaches and trip leaders.

Working with Stage Three Adolescents

In the third stage of adolescent leadership development, the focus turns inward. Adolescents work on being leaders in small ways in areas of importance to them. Often, the ultimate level of leadership development is thought to be achieved when people, both adults and adolescents, assume formal leadership roles in organizations. We disagree. For adolescents, we argue that the highest desirable level is when the young person is competent within areas and activities of his life that are of personal importance. The advantage of this is that it grounds the adolescent, providing him with natural support systems.

Leadership development is a unique experience for each adolescent; every individual follows his or her own path. Damian is a good example of an adolescent who developed into a strong leader through his teenage years and was able to enter adulthood with a firm set of skills and beliefs. The path does not follow a straight line, nor is it easy. In Damian's case, he often took two steps ahead and then fell three steps back. Trying to predict the end result of an adolescent's development is a futile exercise, because leadership development is an ongoing process.

Adults continue to be important in Stage Three of leadership development. In fact, adults play numerous roles. They are *partners* when they share an interest with an adolescent; it could be academic, athletic, artistic, recreational, or vocational. Oftentimes as adolescents pursue their interests, they meet adults and other adolescents who share a fascination. These individuals can act as *mentors* to the young people as they pursue their interest. Adults are also *resources* for teenagers. They provide emotional support and access to knowledge that the youths require. Adults are also *role models* for adolescents, setting examples, providing feedback, and helping them pursue their dreams.

Even at this level, we encourage adults to seek out adolescents to talk individually and in group settings about how the youths are performing leadership tasks and being leaders in their own lives. Reflection on what adolescents are doing and learning is critical in this stage of leadership development. Since everyone is familiar with group process and expectations, adults join the conversations as colleagues and mentors. The adolescents themselves can take responsibility for finding a place to meet and informing others of the date and time of the meeting. These meetings provide an opportunity for celebration and recognition of accomplishments. They also provide support when help is needed. The meetings are a grounding time; they help remind the teens of the fundamentals of leadership. They are opportunities to openly discuss what is working and what isn't in their activities.

Adults help adolescents in Stage Three to be realistic about what they are able to do and what they still need to achieve. Adults help them confront the reality that they cannot function at the level of Stage Three in every area of their lives. The concept of not living entirely in Stage Three is critical. Much of the work of the adults is meant to help adolescents gain a sense of balance and control in their lives, while not losing their creativity, spontaneity, and energy. The goal for adolescents in Stage Three is not to be *busy* as they were in Stage Two, but instead to be *focused*. Going back and working on basic communication, decision-making, and stress-management skills is one way adults help adolescents maintain their focus.

Helping adolescents to be focused as they pursue their interests requires effort in a number of areas (Figure 6.1). The balance between transactional and transformational leadership skills continues to be important. We don't want youths taking on lots of activities without any focus as to why they're involved. It is okay for adolescents to participate, but in Stage Three we need to help them focus their interest, energy, and creativity.

Adults working with Stage Three adolescents often feel as though they are sitting on the sidelines, but they should never underestimate the importance of their support and encouragement.

Leadership Information

Adolescents in Stage Three have internalized the leadership information that was first introduced in Stage One; they are unconsciously able to incorporate this knowledge into their behavior. They now understand the components necessary for groups to work well together. For an adult working with Stage Three adolescents, it is important to notice and compliment them when they demonstrate their ability to facilitate a group. Stage Three adolescents are

Figure 6.1 Stage Three Focus Areas

	Transformational	*Transactional*
Leadership Information	Internalizing • Group expectations • Group dynamics • Group stages • Experiential learning	Focusing attention Locating resources Completing projects
Leadership Attitude	Vision Competence	Requesting feedback Working toward goals

Communication Skills	Processing thoughts and
	   feelings effectively
	Using active listening
		Expressing thoughts
		   successfully, both in
		   writing and verbally

Decision-Making Skills	Higher levels of decision
	   making; considering
	   alternatives and being
	   aware of their uncertainty
		Regularly evaluating
		   decisions already made

Stress-Management Skills	Monitoring the need to
	   increase or decrease
	   stress
		Routinely practicing
		   methods of managing
		   stress

becoming young colleagues who are capable (with some good coaching) of accomplishing much.

The transactional leadership skills that need attention at this time are organizing support and locating resources. Stage Three youth need help to focus their attention in specific areas. This requires compiling information, perhaps in several areas before finally making a major decision. Adults can help youths locate resources, while also encouraging them to search on their own.

Leadership Attitude

Transformational leadership attitudes involve competence and vision. Adults can support adolescents in honing the skills that help them increase their competence in areas of interest to them. When Stage Three youths reach competence, they begin to imagine what they can possibly enjoy and be good at in the future.

Adults can help young people by giving them honest feedback about their strengths and weakness. It isn't good to give adolescents an overly optimistic view of their capabilities. On the other hand, when they demonstrate real skills, they should be recognized and praised. Adults should also be ready to receive positive and negative feedback from time to time. How an adult responds to this feedback shows the adolescent how to accept positive and negative feedback and use the advice constructively.

Working with Stage Three adolescents also involves helping them strive for their goals. Reminding them to think about the goals they have set for themselves is a helpful way for them to stay focused.

Communication Skills

Adults working with Stage Three adolescents can model good understanding of communication, and of active listening so that youths know what it entails. According to McKay, Davis, and Fanning, "Active listening is a commitment and a compliment. It's a commitment to understand how other people feel, how they see their world. It means putting aside your own prejudices and beliefs, your anxieties and self-interest, so that you can step behind the other person's eyes. You try to look at things from his or her perspective. Listening is a compliment because it says to the other person: 'I care about what is happening to you; your life and your experience are important'" (1983, p. 14).

Active listening is such an important component of communication because without it trouble can be right around the next corner. When individuals don't actively listen, important information is missed and problems are not foreseen. Adults can help Stage Three youths head off imminent difficulties.

Try to be nonjudgmental so that adolescents can safely tell you what they are thinking, even if their thoughts are unusual. It is very meaningful to them when an adult values and responds seriously to their ideas.

Adults can help youth express thoughts successfully, both verbally and in writing. We can seek, or create, opportunities for adolescents to collect their thoughts and speak out. Often a local foundation or service organization requests a youth panel at a meeting so as to be brought up to date on what is happening with the young people in the community. Some opportunities are more permanent, as with the ACE program discussed in Chapter Ten. We can also encourage young people to write to the editor of the local newspaper when they are interested in a community issue. Stage Three adolescents express themselves in many surprising ways: through drama, poetry, and service projects.

Decision-Making Skills

Higher-level decision making takes place constantly among Stage Three adolescents. Pressure is mounting for these young people to make decisions about what to do when they graduate from high school; they must decide among college, military service, a job, and other paths. They have to consider the expectations of many different people when they make such a choice: their parents, teachers, coaches, friends, and so on. The pressure is sometimes overwhelming, and the decisions often seem too big to make. Adults can "silently" help by being available and offering information when asked. It is not likely that Stage Three adolescents will allow adults to assume responsibility for decisions about their future. Adults should trust at this point that they have supplied the support and guidance that allow the young person to act wisely.

Stage Three adolescents often ask adults to help them evaluate their decisions once they have been made. This is a time to exercise restraint and to actively listen to adolescents, letting them know you are interested in their decisions.

Stress-Management Skills

Adults working with Stage Three adolescents probably require more stress management than the adolescents do! Stage Three adolescents have learned to monitor their need to increase or decrease stress. Sometimes stress must be increased so that an adolescent is motivated to get things done or take a risk, such as going on a job interview or asking someone out on a date. This is positive stress that is understood to be constructive. At other times, stress needs to be decreased, as when adolescents take on too many activities and begin to have trouble focusing clearly on their original goals. Adults can help by showing youths how to assess their activity levels and perfect their coping strategies.

Adults can also help adolescents balance work and play. Organizing events just to have fun and reducing the competitiveness of activities helps adolescents relax and shows them how to take the work out of a social event. Stage Three teens need places where they can just be themselves comfortably, and adults can help them find such places.

Reflections on Stage Three: Stepping Up

Stage Three leadership is about stepping forward and being seen. It is the gathering and focusing of energy that allows adolescents to step into a new role in one area of their lives. It involves preparation and support. It can be full of anxiety, self-doubt, and resistance, but is also highly fulfilling. In this stage, ordinary adolescents realize that they have an interest, ability, or desire that can propel them to another level of development and discovery. In Stage Three, adolescents are actually directing their lives. They are leaders.

Part Three

Strategies for Leadership Development

Nurturing adolescent leaders involves engaging youths in new roles. Adults—be they parents, teachers, community agency staff, employers, principals, clergy, or neighbors—interact with adolescents in new ways. This is challenging and sometimes even seems impossible. Adolescents spend a tremendous amount of time with other adolescents. They're together in school and they hang out after school; at night and on weekends, they are together again. As they get older, they may work at the same place. They talk on the telephone, often making further mutual plans. One reason that they have such a drive to be with others of their own age is that they are all going through the same process: a process in which they give up their childhood roles and try out new roles to carry into adulthood. They are all anxious about whether they will be ready when the time comes for them to assume adult responsibilities in society (Ianni, 1989, pp. 22–23).

Working with adolescents to develop their leadership potential and abilities obliges adults to enter the world where youths live. We have to know and understand them; discover their perceptions, beliefs, and values; and find out what motivates them. Then we can build the capacity of our schools and communities to work with young people to develop both transactional and transformational leadership.

In the final four chapters of this book, we explore how to motivate and support leadership development. We switch our focus from teenagers to adults and look at a range of activities and tasks that can be undertaken to nurture adolescent leaders. Leadership is a social process. For adolescents to fully develop their leadership potential, they need adult support. The following chapters focus on what adults can do to provide this support.

Chapter Seven

How Adults Can Nurture Leadership Development

When we first became involved in youth leadership development, our instinct was to start the work with the adolescents themselves. We set up workshops and programs to teach teenagers how to be leaders. We talked, worked on projects, and did recreational activities with adolescents. While these experiences were fun and rewarding, they did not achieve our intended goals.

We realized that we needed to go back to square one. We had to take time to study ourselves, our organizations, and our communities to come to a real understanding of where youth leadership fits into our lives. We couldn't be effective in working with young people until we understood our own views on transformational and transactional leadership. Likewise, we needed to appreciate the challenges adults, particularly parents, face in developing the leadership potential of adolescents. Finally, we had to look at the power of groups in the lives of adolescents. Adolescents spend their lives with people in groups (families, peers, recreation, work). Understanding how groups work and the power of reflection as part of the group process provided us with essential tools to help teenagers assess and evaluate their leadership development.

In this chapter we explore our own leadership information, attitudes, motivations, and expectations. We then look at how to support our colleagues and parents of teenagers to facilitate leadership development of adolescents. We discuss groups as a powerful tool for helping adolescents see themselves as leaders and talk about how teenagers can use reflection as part of the group experience to assess their leadership development. Once we have gained such knowledge, we are equipped to work with adolescents in developing leadership potential.

Challenging Ourselves

We assume that since you are reading this book, you probably already work with teenagers or are a parent or community member interested in adolescents. You may be a teacher, counselor, social worker, youth worker, member of the clergy, coach, employer, nurse, or physician. Once you become involved in adolescent leadership development, you accept certain obligations. You might have some idea of what to expect: what you'll be doing, who you'll be working with, and what must be accomplished.

You also have the right to have your expectations met, and to use your skills and knowledge in a way that ensures that your time is not wasted. But you should be clear about your expectations and assumptions and decide whether they are realistic. This is especially important because, as a way of enticing people to participate, school principals, agency directors, and community leaders sometimes understate the amount of time and effort involved.

It is helpful to spend some time thinking about why you want to be (or already are) involved with leadership development. Be aware of your motivations, and recognize the fact that they may change. In the beginning many people's primary reason for being involved is to work with a particular group of young people. They often find the experience so enjoyable that they want to continue even after those young people have moved on in life. Figure 7.1 is a list of some common reasons people give for their involvement in leadership development. Take time to consider which of these are incentives for your own involvement.

Next we suggest you think about what you expect and what is expected of you as you work in leadership development. What strengths, skills, experience, and knowledge do you bring to the experience? Which tasks, activities, and responsibilities do you expect to enjoy the most, and which the least? What needs to hap-

Figure 7.1 Why Am I Involved?

To maintain and increase skills.

To advance my career.

To promote adolescents as leaders.

To make decisions that may influence my organization.

My family believes youth leadership development is important.

It's a job requirement.

I'm responding to a direct request that I participate.

The work will not be done otherwise.

To explore a new way to work with adolescents.

To change the way community members and parents view adolescents.

I like working with teenagers.

To establish contacts in the school and community.

To assume leadership responsibilities.

To help all teenagers realize their leadership potential.

To improve school and community relations.

pen for you to be satisfied? What do you hope to accomplish through your work?

These questions are designed to help you think about your motivation to work with adolescents. What makes these questions critical is that the type of leadership development we propose does not involve working with a select group of predetermined youth based on their participation in formal school and community activities; we do not include only the class officers, youth group leaders, and athletic team captains. Instead, our model of leadership development includes all youths, and many of them may be anxious about their leadership abilities and resistant to exploring their potential as leaders.

To work in any area of youth development requires responsibility and energy. Many of those involved report increased participation in activities, more commitments, and greater time constraints. These people are often identified by others in their organizations and communities as leaders in working with youth.

They frequently find themselves taking on the role of youth advocate and champion. They may be comfortable in this role, or, depending on their experience, they may need time to become accustomed to it.

This work also requires that you internalize the concepts of transformational and transactional leadership. If you are to help develop the leadership potential of youth, you must first look at your own development as a leader. How do you act as a leader in your own daily life? Notice that we do not say you should ask yourself, "Am I a leader?" This is because we believe that all people have leadership potential and demonstrate leadership in big and small ways in many situations. Do you agree? Is it hard for you to picture yourself as a leader? Do you believe in your leadership ability? Take time to think about these questions. The adolescents you work with are struggling with the very same questions. They'll ask you if you are a leader; confessing that you struggle over this question yourself is a good way of helping them appreciate the difficulties involved in developing leadership potential and abilities.

Answering these questions is just the beginning. As we have pointed out, there is more than one type of leadership, so there is more to consider. What does it mean to be a transformational leader? What does it mean to be a transactional leader? Figure 7.2 illustrates some of the visions, focus, and approaches related to these two types of leadership. Reflect on situations where you act as a transformational or a transactional leader; both types of leadership are important. Reflection helps profoundly in working with youth to develop leadership potential.

Adults in the World of Adolescents

It is a challenge to live with, teach, and work with adolescents. At any given moment, they may test limits or take action without considering the consequences of their behavior. For adults, adolescents can be a great source of anxiety, pride, frustration, and joy. Probably the biggest challenge for adults working in the area of adoles-

Figure 7.2 Transformational and Transactional Leaders

Transformational

Vision	Focus	Approach
Values the participation and contribution of others	Development of self first to be a better contributor to the group	Open-minded
Takes into account all things people have said and then decides	Ongoing learning from experiences to generalize to "real life"	Creative in integrating people's ideas
Considers individuals in their context and situation	Shared leadership; group power	Flexible
Uses individuals to test decisions	Sees the process as important	Supportive

Transactional

Vision	Focus	Approach
Values problem and solution identification	Development of self to be a better decision maker for the group	Persuasive
Makes decisions—even if everyone has not been heard—in order to move forward	Gets things done	Creative in developing new ideas
Uses standards and principles as guides in decision making	Sees the product as important	Use of time management
	Takes charge; personal power	

cent leadership development is to provide teenagers with the support and guidance they need, while not blocking or restricting their individual growth.

Communication with adolescents can be highly problematic. Teenagers frequently come into conflict with adults as they develop their individuality. They learn to voice their opinions in a variety situations every day, discovering how to speak for themselves right under our noses: on the street corner, in the classroom, at home, on the football field, at a chess club meeting, and just about anywhere teens gather. Through practice and experience, teens learn how they can and cannot affect their world. When adolescents express opinions differing from other people's (especially adults'), adults frequently view this as troublesome or argumentative behavior. When this sort of conflict arises, teens sometimes assume that adults are objecting to the *fact* that their opinion is different, not to the *quality* of that opinion. In such a situation, teens usually exhibit one of two behaviors: they stop voicing their opinions, or they become even more vocal than before.

One of the key distinctions between being argumentative for its own sake and expressing a difference of opinion is in the delivery and reception of the message. If the adolescent can send the message in a manner that can be accepted by the adult, then the teen's idea may be viewed as a reasonable—possibly even a valuable—idea. When a difference of opinion is delivered with an "attitude," it is instead viewed as troublesome. The challenge for adults is to avoid getting caught up in adolescents' communication struggles.

The flip side is that adults also need to take responsibility for their own communication skills. This means recognizing that we, too, are often wrong and can sometimes speak in a way that makes teenagers feel patronized, defensive, or possibly even belittled and embarrassed. We must also accept that adolescents' ideas and opinions can flow in a trickle or a tidal wave, and learning to manage this flow is what adolescence is all about. Knowing this helps foster patience with teens as they learn to communicate effectively.

A second challenge for adults who work with adolescents is to understand that many youths find it very difficult to behave consistently. Older adolescents may say they want to work and then successfully obtain a job. Most teenagers, though, have trouble getting a job, and if they encounter obstacles they give up trying. This can be frustrating for teenagers and adults both, which is a critical point for adults who work with adolescents. Adults often become frustrated with a teenager's delays, excuses, procrastination, and wasted time; adolescents say they want one thing, but their subsequent actions show no evidence to support their statements. Their behavior is inconsistent with their words, and the message to adults is that the teenagers themselves are inconsistent, irresponsible, and untrustworthy. As adolescent behavior begins to match beliefs and attitudes, adults and peers alike start to see the young people as credible and self-assured; eventually the adolescents themselves come to believe they have these qualities. But it is a long and frustrating path to reach that point.

Supporting leadership behavior in adolescents is easy for adults if the behavior is seen as positive. When adolescents do something out of the ordinary and it has a positive outcome, it is easy to encourage and congratulate their effort. If their effort to use leadership skills has a less-than-positive outcome, it is difficult for adults to see the benefit.

Jorge, a junior in high school, was invited to attend meetings of the school board. Little was required of him other than attending meetings and speaking when he was spoken to, which was infrequent. At the final meeting of the school year, Jorge was asked for his opinion; he told the board about the issues that were important to him. They centered on daily life at the high school: things like smoking, dirty restrooms, poor lunches, and unfair teachers. The board was mortified. This was not the kind of leadership they had in mind when they invited a student to be present at meetings. Jorge understood their reaction to mean that the board didn't really want to hear his opinion. His ideas would have been better received had he worded his message differently, but that was not what Jorge was left to reflect on. He was made to feel that the board found these issues unimportant, and that he had shown very poor judgment in choosing a forum to air his complaints.

Often adults invite adolescents' opinions, only to decide afterward what to respond to and what to ignore. This is worse than not asking for their opinion at all. Adolescents learn much of what they know about leadership from the adults in their world. Probably the most important message adults can give teens is that they believe adolescents can be valuable leaders who have influence over what happens in their lives, their families, the school, the community, and beyond.

Parents as Partners in Leadership Development

Parents and teenagers talk about lots of things. Evening conversations cover topics ranging from substitute teachers, behavior in class, homework assignments, friends, and what they ate for lunch, to after-school activities, their job, and upcoming parties and weekend events. Frequently, parents get to share details about their work: customers, meetings, their supervisor, and so on. In fact, with so many other aspects of life to discuss, it is possible that parents never get to talk to their children about leaders and leadership. This is not a regular topic of conversation between parents and adolescents. If parents visit school, they are more likely to talk to teachers about their child's academic performance or behavior in class than about leadership development. Any contact or information a parent does have concerning leadership development activities most likely comes as part of an initial school visit, community youth program orientation, or parent night. Occasionally parents are invited to attend an event where their adolescent receives recognition for his leadership ability. But this is rare; it is equally rare for large numbers of parents—particularly parents of teenagers—to be involved with such school activities through a leadership team. Those parents who are involved usually happen to be in a related profession such as coaching, teaching, or counseling.

When we talk with parents, they generally have a positive outlook on youth leadership development. They're just not sure if *their* child is a leader. They believe that schools, jobs, agencies, and community activities may help develop adolescents' leadership potential; they believe that at least these activities don't *hurt* their children. Parents' perceptions are often based on their own childhood and adolescent leadership experiences, or lack thereof. These experiences provide parents with a frame of reference. They might have very unpleasant memories. Some parents may have exhibited behavior problems or had special education needs when they were in school, and so they were never exposed to leadership opportunities. As discussed earlier, most adults themselves struggle with the concepts of leadership and leaders. This confusion carries over into their relationship with their children. The consequence of the confusion is that parents are often uncertain about youth leadership development and opportunities. They may have incorrect information or no information at all.

Parents are not sure why they should become involved with leadership development. For most parents, no clear connection exists between leadership development activities and their adolescent's success socially or in school, sports, or work. Classroom teachers, employers, and sports coaches are people whom parents might come into contact with and whom they see working with their children day in and day out. In most cases, though, these people teach adolescents traditional things in the traditional way; at work, for instance, teenagers learn job skills, though initially they are mostly low-skill tasks.

Leadership is not something parents see their child learning. Parents are sometimes even wary that it could get in the way of their child's "real" education. However, the concept of developing their child's leadership potential and abilities usually holds a certain appeal for parents. In fact, few would say that they do not support such activity. Even so, most parents probably see it as an extra. They give higher priority to their children finishing high school with the best grades possible; to their attending a postsecondary educational institution; and to such issues as personal safety, health, positive relationships, and employment. Being involved with leadership development activities would be OK, but parents believe the time would be better spent in other areas such as helping their children stay in school and get better grades.

The situation is exacerbated if parents think schools, agencies, youth groups, employers, and even the adolescents themselves do not want them (the parents) to be involved in the leadership development. Parents report that they feel nervous about participating in the school, work, and community lives of their adolescent. Parental involvement may be limited to attending a few school events, driving their child to activities and work, and involving friends of their adolescent in family activities. Parents see a boundary between themselves and teachers and employers. Many parents don't see themselves talking to their teenager's employer about more job responsibility and possible leadership opportunities. Rather, parents see themselves supporting and helping their child speak for herself to her employer or teacher. Parents clearly see a boundary to their involvement.

The best strategies for involving parents actually come from adolescents themselves. Clearly, we can encourage leadership as a topic of family conversation. Furthermore, we can design programs and newsletters to link leadership development to student success in schools, communities, and workplaces. However, in our talks with adolescents about how their parents might help them to be leaders, adolescents identify two critical roles for parents (which fact essentially answers the parental question about involvement). Teenagers talk about their parents as being supporters who contribute guidance and resources, and role models who demonstrate leadership attitudes and skills.

Teenagers want to feel that their parents believe and behave as though they (the adolescents) are capable of being leaders. The message that teenagers too often report is that their parents perceive them as good people but not leaders. Parents provide lots of feedback to their children. We want parents to include in this feedback some praise for their child wherever he has demonstrated leadership. Working with parents to encourage and support adolescents as they question their leadership abilities goes far toward supporting leadership development.

Probably the most powerful influence parents can have in adolescent leadership development is as role models. Actions do speak louder than words for most teenagers, and parental involvement in community, social, business, school, and family activities provides an opportunity for adults to model leadership within their own lives. Parents can share experiences with their children and talk about how they resolved their own conflicts and challenges. Many leadership opportunities exist for parents—although they too may need help locating them. Like adolescents, they have trouble believing in their own leadership abilities. Workshops that target parents strengthen and nurture a leadership environment for everyone.

Leadership among adolescents grows and is sustained through parents' actions and support. Their involvement as role models and supporters of leadership extends beyond their own child's years in school. Supporting parents as part of the process supports leadership as a family value over a lifetime.

Groups and Adolescents

Family groups, peer groups, social groups, and school groups are all part of an adolescent's life. The approval of a group of peers is a powerful source of motivation and support for teens who are learning new skills.

Leadership is a social process; it involves interaction with other people. It occurs in groups of people; therefore, using educational groups—groups focused on skill acquisition—in leadership development allows teenagers the opportunity to learn and practice their skills in a safe yet realistic environment. The use of groups in developing adolescent leadership is very beneficial. The group should make a point of showing recognition and approval to those members who are serious in their effort to improve leadership skills. The more an adolescent practices his leadership skills, the more group approval he should receive. The progress of every group member is enhanced if the group supports all participants' attempts to experiment with new behavior and take risks by trying out their new skills. There are few influences on adolescents' behavior that are more powerful than the support and approval of their peers.

Using education groups to facilitate adolescent development is one of the most constructive ways to ensure that teens increase their leadership skills. Initially, it is a way of paying special attention to leadership development, offering a new mode of learning that adds intensity to the experience. Over time, it becomes a safe environment for receiving and giving feedback and practicing new behaviors. Most teachers and many community agency staff are not prepared to work with adolescents in educational groups. This is often viewed as a deficiency on the part of teachers and staff members. However, working with students in educational groups is a technique that can be learned, and when the technique is used correctly it can be an extremely effective educational methodology to help facilitate leadership development. In Chapter Nine we discuss the details of learning how to use educational groups.

In this section we focus on what adolescents need to know about groups; to work effectively in groups, the adolescents themselves must understand the group process. Information on that process provides a basis on which they can apply what they experience in groups to real-life situations. This information is not enough by itself for adolescents to make the connection between educational experience and real life, but through activities and discussions they are better able to see how the information can be used. Group process focuses on four key pieces of information: group expectations, group dynamics, the stages of a group, and experiential learning. As a final part of our discussion on educational groups, we talk about experiential learning and in particular the process of reflection that we suggest teenagers use to assess their leadership development.

Group Expectations

Adolescents know that there are unwritten rules in the groups they belong to. Their families have rules, their friends have rules, and their classes have rules. The rules are usually not explicit; adolescents learn to follow them by being corrected after making a mistake. This is a difficult way to find out what is expected of them. Building a list of expectations when each group first comes together provides an opportunity for youths to see exactly what it is they are being asked to do. Following are some suggestions of reasonable expectations for any type of group:

Accept others' feelings and thoughts; agreement is not necessary.
Often adolescents believe that they must agree with everyone to be
accepted. When they don't agree, they don't know how to express
disagreement positively. Teens often go along with the crowd in
order to be accepted. It is important to emphasize that disagreement is OK and should be expected. Being able to disagree and not
be criticized for it is often a new experience for an adolescent.

Speak for yourself; use "I" statements. Owning statements is
sometimes hard because it puts a person at risk of disagreement
from others. Both adults and adolescents favor "you think" or "we
meant," speaking in the second or third person to avoid going out
on a limb themselves. Using the word *I* when making statements
(that is, speaking in the first person) and speaking directly to a person is the key to following this ground rule.

Avoid put-downs. Put-downs are the most powerful way for a
participant to squelch a group. Group trust fades fast or simply
never forms if put-downs are allowed. It is important to be explicit
about what is considered a put-down; inside jokes, not paying
attention to speakers, and leaving people out are just a few examples. Teens often justify put-downs by joking that they don't really
mean it. It is important to emphasize that put-downs hurt even
when the person laughs it off.

Take responsibility for your own learning. The leadership development model discussed in this book is a facilitated model, not one
that is taught. Therefore, students are encouraged to take responsibility for paying attention, sharing what they learn from others,
and planning how they might use this experience in their own
lives. There is a direct correlation between what is put into the
experience (commitment, energy, and enthusiasm) and what is
gained from it (knowledge, practice, and increased skill level).

Be open to participation; you have the option to pass. Encourage
participants to try new things and take some appropriate risks
to advance their learning. But they should always have the option to
pass on an activity. This allows an individual to make a decision

about whether and how she would like to participate. Often physical problems hinder participation. Alternative roles should be arranged for anyone not directly participating. Make sure each participant has a role, and emphasize that each person is an important member of the group.

Respect confidentiality. "Confidential" is often taken to mean "secret"—by students and adults alike. Here, *confidentiality* does not mean keeping people's secrets, but rather respecting their right to express their thoughts and feelings without worrying that someone will talk about them outside of the group. Take the time to explain why confidentiality is essential in building group trust.

These group expectations should become a standard part of each activity and program and should be enforced in the beginning of every group experience. This can be done in a way that is not embarrassing or humiliating to the offender and yet is direct. It is important that adolescents see adults enforcing expectations in a constructive, nonalienating manner so that they know it is possible to confront positively. At first this may seem artificial, but it soon becomes internalized by the adolescents and they begin to correct their peers when they see them violating a group expectation. This is one of the most fundamental ingredients in creating an atmosphere that nurtures transformational leadership development.

Group Dynamics

As individuals begin to work in groups, they discover that there are patterns of group development; they learn that all groups develop in predictable ways. Information about group development and dynamics dispels myths about groups. One myth many adolescents believe is that "nobody feels the way I do." Feelings of isolation and detachment are common among individuals who enter a new group. As adolescents learn more about the tasks necessary for groups to evolve, they discover that there is more to forming a positively functioning group than just bringing people together.

Adolescents learn why people have come to the group. Through activities, participants share what they are feeling and why they are there. Sometimes the primary reason why adolescents participate is that their parents want them to, so there can be some resistance or indifference on the part of participants in the beginning. Once you know the reasons behind their attitudes, however, it becomes much easier to understand and accept their behavior.

As adolescents discover how groups operate, and as they learn about the kinds of forces that exist within groups, they begin to understand how they can fit into their own groups.

The Stages of a Group

Learning about the stages a group progresses through (Figure 7.3) is important because it helps adolescents prepare to work effectively with others. A group must complete a task within each stage before it can move on to the next step. The planning stage is one of gathering information and deciding to go or not to go to a new group experience. Once trust (the initial stage) has been established, confrontation (the transitional stage) takes place. How confrontations are handled often determines how the group continues to progress through the stages. Cohesion (the working stage) shows that a group is working well: all participants are playing an equal role in the group. Reaching cohesion means that a group has accomplished its goal to achieve a positive group experience. Cohesion only takes place after a group has worked through all of the stages that precede it, including confrontation. Termination (the final stage) completes the group experience.

The planning, initial, and final stages take place automatically in every group experience. It is up to the group participants and their facilitator to work through the other stages. All groups pass through the stages at different speeds and to differing degrees. Groups may also regress to previous stages at the onset of a new task—or even with the addition or departure of one or more group participants.

Figure 7.3 The Stages of a Group

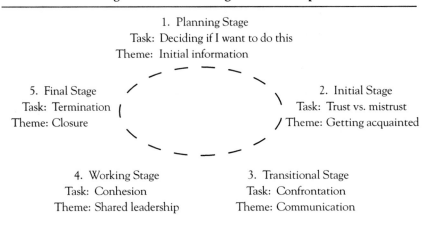

1. Planning Stage
Task: Deciding if I want to do this
Theme: Initial information

5. Final Stage
Task: Termination
Theme: Closure

2. Initial Stage
Task: Trust vs. mistrust
Theme: Getting acquainted

4. Working Stage
Task: Conhesion
Theme: Shared leadership

3. Transitional Stage
Task: Confrontation
Theme: Communication

Understanding the stages of a group is confusing for adolescents, because the information is not very tangible or concrete. We ask adolescents to recall a time when they felt a genuine sense of belonging, a time when trust was high. Some adolescents have had that experience and some haven't. Those who have often recall the hard work that was necessary to get to that point.

Understanding that the working stage is not reached without enduring a time-consuming process that includes confrontation helps to at least predict a group's road to cohesion, if not make it easier.

Experiential Learning

Experiential learning only happens when a person participates in an activity and then looks back at the experience critically, gains some useful insight from analyzing it, and puts the resulting knowledge to work in his everyday life. Each phase of this process (Figure 7.4) is critical to turning an activity into experiential learning.

The cyclical experiential learning process is a new way for adolescents to look at learning. In the setting of a program or activity, adolescents are guided through experiences that are enjoyable but also illustrate points about leadership. Participants are asked to

Figure 7.4 Phases of the Experiential Learning Cycle

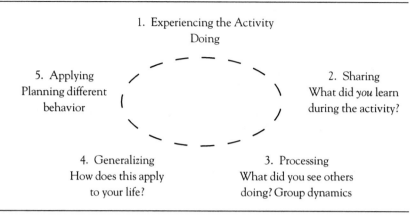

1. Experiencing the Activity
Doing

5. Applying
Planning different
behavior

2. Sharing
What did *you* learn
during the activity?

4. Generalizing
How does this apply
to your life?

3. Processing
What did you see others
doing? Group dynamics

share their individual responses to the experiences, as well as to observe and report what they see happening among group members. This helps participants to practice thinking in a way that lets them use the experiential learning model to gain knowledge from every experience in their lives. Different points of view are encouraged, giving adolescents the benefit of their peers' observations as well as their own. At first, experiential learning takes place only during structured activities. Time and practice allow this type of learning to be internalized, however, and adolescents are then able to learn leadership from everything they do. This becomes a powerful way for students to gain knowledge in their everyday lives.

The goal of any experiential learning activity is for the responsibility of learning to be transferred from the facilitator to the participants. This is especially important for adolescents because they need to feel they have power over their lives; taking responsibility for their learning helps give them that power. Young people become aware of their own contributions to the activity, as well as the contributions of others. Sharing their individual reactions to activities as well as observing and reporting the interactions within the group are often new experiences for young people. This is why it's so important that they be given a strong theoretical base to explain why they should make an effort to try this different way of learning. When the experiential learning model is used consistently, adolescents become more comfortable with it and are able to greatly enhance their skills.

Each phase is equally important to learning. Often, so much attention is paid to the doing part of an activity or project that all other parts are neglected. The actual task at hand is the focus of most preparation, because before anything happens the materials must be gathered, the location secured, and the directions clearly administered. As a result, other aspects of activities are often not planned, and the opportunity to gain some lasting, critical knowledge from the experience slips away.

It is important to note that the fourth and fifth phases of the experiential learning method, that is, generalizing and applying the learning, sometimes take place during the leadership experience itself, but most often they happen sometime later. It is necessary for the entire cycle to be completed for learning to be internalized and incorporated into an individual's repertoire of behavior. As situations present themselves in the "real world," adolescents try out new behavior they have learned.

An experiential learning environment that is supported by adults allows young people to test their budding skills. Adults need to recognize that practicing the leadership skills being learned helps adolescents discover for themselves how to balance leading and following with their peers. By modeling appropriate behavior, adults can demonstrate the give-and-take that is integral to leadership.

Reflection as Leadership Assessment

We are often asked to provide instruments, tests, and measures to assess adolescent leadership development. What teachers, parents, counselors, agency staff, and even adolescents want is a paper-and-pencil tool that they can use to measure leadership. There are many such measures of adult leadership development, and they reflect dozens of underlying theories (Bass, 1990). From our point of view, there are at least two problems with the leadership measures that are currently available. First, they focus primarily on adults, and are therefore inappropriate as measures of adolescent leadership. Second, they tend to concentrate on leadership in formal organizations, such as businesses and the armed services, which is highly limiting. Sometimes, however (depending on the particular situation, project, or adolescents involved), a given measure may be worthwhile and perhaps be adapted to fit the case at hand.

Assessment of participants' progress is an essential part of leadership development. At times we design and use paper-and-pencil tests, written reports, and oral presentations to appraise their development.

For the most part, however, we use the experiential learning process of reflection: looking back at an experience critically, gaining useful insight from analyzing it, and putting the resulting knowledge to work in everyday life. Reflection involves active, persistent, and careful consideration by teens regarding their knowledge, attitudes, and behavior (Fertman, 1994). Reflection means asking questions such as "What am I doing?" "Why am I doing it?" and "What am I learning?" We help teenagers reflect on how they are "doing leadership" and " being leaders." Reflection gives them an understanding of the meaning and impact of their efforts to develop their leadership potential. Without reflection, adolescents do not integrate what they experience.

Reflection is part of each phase of the experiential learning process. Often as part of the leadership development reflection process, adolescents maintain a journal; we encourage participants to speak and write about their experiences. The forms of reflection are not limited to speaking and writing. For example, students can create portfolios of leadership experiences and materials or use multimedia to demonstrate and assess their leadership development. Reflection involves thinking, but it is more than simply bringing something to mind; during a period of reflection, adolescents meditate, muse, contemplate, ponder, deliberate, cogitate, reason, and speculate. The goal of reflection is to achieve a higher level of thinking (Fertman, White, and White, 1996).

While there are many effective forms of reflection (Toole and Toole, 1995), several fundamental elements are present in high-quality reflection. First, reflection should be structured; it should have a clear objective. For example, when we work with teens in Stage One of leadership development, we are clear about the information and skills we want them to gain. Our reflections focus on determining whether or not the teenagers have acquired the desired information and skills. Second, the method selected should be consistent with the adolescent's work. For instance, journal-writing fosters personal growth, and small group discussions are effective for feedback on communication skills. Third, reflection should be ongoing. It should be made a part of every activity and experience.

The case studies in Chapters Four, Five, and Six can help adults understand and recognize the stages of leadership development and chart an adolescent's leadership development. However, reflection by the youth provides a personal assessment and a powerful tool for plotting his or her leadership development. To help structure the reflection, we have designed leadership reflection guides for each stage, based on the focus areas of each stage discussed in Chapters Four, Five, and Six. There are two guides per stage, one focused on transformational leadership and one focused on transactional leadership. An example of a reflection guide for Stage One transformational focus areas is shown in Figure 7.5.

The reflection guides are multipurpose. Teenagers can use them for self-assessments. The guides can also be completed by adults (teachers, parents, youth workers) and peers to provide additional information and data. When regularly collected and compiled, data from the guides can be effective in charting individual adolescents' leadership development.

Figure 7.5 Sample Reflection Guide: Stage One Transformational Focus Areas

Reflection Guide: Stage One Transformational Focus Areas

	Instructions: Using the ratings (1, 2, or 3), please assess each leadership focus area's importance to you and your proficiency in that area	*Importance* (1 = low; 2 = moderate; 3 = high)	*Proficiency* (1 = low; 2 = moderate; 3 = high)
Leadership Information	Group expectations Group dynamics Group stages Experiential learning		
Leadership Attitude	Awareness of personal leadership Being kind and fair to peers		
Communication Skills	Distinctions made between aggressiveness, assertiveness, and passivity		
Decision-Making Skills	Awareness of decision making as a leadership quality Understanding how belief system affects decisions Shared decision making		
Stress-Management Skills	Identifying personal stress		

Name:

Date:

Chapter Eight

What Organizations and Communities Can Do

In this chapter, we explore ways to motivate and support leadership development within an adolescent's world. Our goal is to create supportive and challenging environments within which young people can develop and explore their leadership potential and abilities. Our strategy is to build on what is already in place in a community and to emphasize adolescents' doing leadership tasks and being leaders. We want others to see adolescents as leaders, by showing that teenagers are in reality leading every day, in big and small ways. At times they are doing leadership: leading discussions, giving directions, talking in small groups. At other times they are being leaders: pursuing interests, producing artwork, working hard. To see adolescents as leaders, we must first understand that leadership opportunities are plentiful and that they are indeed within the reach of most youth. Believing that adolescents can be leaders often means that we must change any perceptions that block this view; many traditional ideas about adolescents interfere with our seeing them as leaders. Changing our perceptions means getting in touch with what helps us see teens as leaders. This chapter focuses on bringing about this change in perception regarding youth leadership and on building support among colleagues to expand their efforts to develop youth leadership.

The Leadership Development Environment

Involving organizations, communities, adults, and adolescents in youth leadership development is no small task. The words *leader* and *leadership* permeate our lives and environments. Leadership is part of the human condition; leaders can be seen among all people, regardless of their culture. Widely held beliefs about who leaders are and how people get to be leaders are socially transmitted and form a person's leadership behavior, knowledge, and attitudes. How a society develops its youth to be leaders is subsumed within these beliefs. Rites-of-passage ceremonies such as high school graduation and religious ceremonies mark the transition from child to responsible adult. Schools offer opportunities for students to be elected student officers, club presidents, and team captains. Youth-serving organizations such as scouts, Campfire, the Ys, 4-H Councils, Boys and Girls Clubs, and Future Farmers offer leadership development activities and programs. These are examples of community-sanctioned opportunities for young people to assume leadership roles in the community. They are manifestations of commonly held beliefs about how adolescents develop leadership abilities in their societies, communities, and families.

These beliefs permeate the world of adolescence. They fill the environments where adolescents spend their time, whether school, family, community, or workplace. One starting point that many people target as they initiate or expand their work in adolescent leadership development is to assess their own organization. What are its beliefs and traditions concerning leadership—in particular, concerning how youths develop their leadership potential and abilities? Assessment of the leadership environment by an organization can help individuals figure out how they can contribute to adolescents' doing leadership tasks and being leaders. Almost every school and youth-serving organization would identify itself, at some level, as developing the leadership potential of adolescents, and it is indeed true that many people and organizations are involved with youth leadership development. However, it is important to focus attention on a number of core characteristics that aid in understanding and realistically estimating the success of youth leadership development efforts.

Every organization has a leadership tradition: a history of developing the leadership potential of the youths it serves. We start by investigating these traditions. There are four key questions:

1. What are the past and current youth leadership development activities?
2. Who was involved in past activities?
3. Who is involved now?
4. What is the motivation behind the leadership activities?

When the staff at Costaño Music and Arts Center asked themselves these questions, they found that their agency had a mixed history. Costaño Music and Arts Center is a community agency with an extensive background in after-school programming for urban youth, and it has certainly included leadership development as part of its mission. However, its leadership programming has been sporadic and has no real niche within the organization. Leadership training there is freestanding, as with such activities as basketball or baby-sitting classes. Leadership is not integrated into the other activities in the program.

The teachers at Jackson High School asked the same questions. They found that their school had a strong history in leadership development, but they discovered some real weaknesses as well. They have a very strong student council system, and its members receive special training each year. The school also has an active National Honor Society, along with successful girls' and boys' basketball teams. These activities are looked on as strong indicators of leadership in the school. The students who were involved in the past are also involved currently and are mostly the academically, athletically, and socially successful group. This means that the bulk of the school population is not involved in the activities that represent leadership to most people. What motivated the leadership activities had a good deal to do with history.

The established activities were part of the fabric of the school, but new activities had a difficult time establishing themselves, and they often struggled for an identity and a place in the school.

Armed with the questions about leadership tradition and benefiting from the brief look at these two institutions, you can take a closer look at the guidance, reinforcement, assistance, and support provided to youth leadership development within your organization and beyond, in other locations: schools, community-based organizations, local government, workplaces, and families. Three levels of indicators assess the strength of a leadership development environment within an organization and beyond in the community itself (Figure 8.1).

Within an organization, we can count the number of staff members, administrators, adolescents, parents, employers, community people, and elected officials working to develop leadership. We can look at the allocation of materials, resources, funding, and education

Figure 8.1 Domains and Indicators of Strength

Domains	Indicators
People	Staff
	Administrators
	Adolescents
	Parents
	Employers
	Community members
	Elected officials
Resources	Materials
	Funding
	Adult leadership education
	Youth leadership education
	Leadership activities
	Leadership opportunities
Vision	Mission statement
	Leadership team

provided by the organization and community. We can look for current leadership activities and opportunities. Finally, we are interested in whether the organizations have (1) created mission statements that focus on leadership and youth development and (2) formed leadership teams to address adolescent leadership development. (Leadership teams are discussed in more detail later in this chapter.)

The information collected for the indicators can range from strictly quantitative data to qualitative reports and reviews. Initially, many communities simply try to determine the presence and quantity of the indicators at each level. This data can then be used to formulate future planning and make decisions. Over time, qualitative data can be collected to assist with decisions related to curriculum design, training, and program development. Strong leadership development environments are consistent and thus provide a solid base on which to build successful programs using strategies that take advantage of the systems for change that already exist within the community.

Assessing the strength of an environment also involves looking at the mix (and levels) of transformational and transactional leadership programs, activities, and opportunities. At first glance, many communities appear to have strong leadership development environments, especially those with school districts offering a full range of extracurricular activities and interscholastic sports. However, we should not be overly impressed with extensive programming and activities. They are to be considered, but we have to determine whether they rely on traditional views of leaders and methods of developing leadership. We wish to find out people's reactions to the concept that all teenagers have leadership potential. Even in the most progressive programs, we do not find universal acceptance of this idea. We should also look at the availability of learning experiences for adolescents, particularly for those in the early stages of leadership development. Are opportunities limited to a small, select group of young people?

We conduct an "action assessment" of the organization. For this, we make queries about student participation in the decision-making process to assess the balance between transformational and transactional leadership. We see the balance as the degree to which adolescents are trusted and held responsible for overseeing and managing the activities of daily life. The continuum of adolescent participation in decision making ranges from none at all to full partnership and consensus in making choices that affect youth (Figure 8.2). Organizations that preclude adolescent participation are seen as using a traditional, transactional model of leadership.

Leadership Environment Scan

A leadership scan is a further assessment of leadership development activities for youth in a community. The scan moves beyond a single organization and looks at the community as a whole: its beliefs, traditions, rites of passage, myths, and celebrations of leaders and leadership. The scan identifies widely held beliefs about who leaders are and how people become leaders. It assesses how the community promotes development of leadership potential in all its members, including adolescents. In many communities a scan is one of the first tasks people join together to complete.

At the most basic level, a scan identifies the range and variety of programs, activities, and opportunities within a community. On a deeper level, it is an opportunity to initiate discussion about how a community develops the skills of its future leaders, its

Figure 8.2 The Role of Adolescents in the Decision-Making Process

Adolescents have *no say* in decisions that affect them.	Select group of adolescents has a *voice* in *student affairs*.	Adolescents have token *membership* in *adult groups*.	*Adolescents and adults* take a majority vote on decisions.	Adolescents and adults reach *consensus* on decisions.

← ————————————————————————————————— →

Environment that inhibits adolescent leaders	Environment that encourages adolescent leaders

youth. Ideally, the scan is a small piece of an ongoing dialogue in a community about youth development. A scan often starts by simply taking inventory. Some inventories are lists of interested and supportive organizations, those involved in youth leadership development. Others include communitywide surveys of youths and adults. As interest develops over time, in-depth information about a community's leadership development environment is sought through a more extensive scan process.

A scan of a leadership development environment involves identifying and clarifying what people believe and envision about adolescent leadership development. Scans typically involve two strategies. The first includes talking individually and in small groups to community leaders, school administrators, parents, adolescents, and colleagues about youth leadership. It is critical to target people who are in a position to affect leadership programming. During discussions with these individuals, we gain information about how a community develops the leadership potential and abilities of its adolescents. The second strategy is to gather standardized information using a number of surveys, as we will discuss later.

Community leaders have varying viewpoints regarding adolescents and leadership development. In the words of the leader of one small town:

> As mayor of my town, I am proud to say that we do everything we can for our kids and do it better than any other community around. We pride ourselves on giving them a well-rounded upbringing through excellent sports and education programs, community service projects, and health and safety programs. Our kids are our future, our top priority; we take their training very seriously and so are interested in improving their chances of future success in any way possible. I think that development of the teenagers' leadership abilities may be just what they need to complete the education we started in their younger days. Encouraging students to run for school elections and to be active in school clubs and activities is one way of molding them into leaders.

The mayor isn't committing any money or resources to develop leadership opportunities, though, and it isn't clear what, if anything, he knows about youth leadership development. We also have no idea from his words whether anything is happening in his schools and community to promote leadership in youth.

Other community leaders, by contrast, are very clear about where leadership development already exists, where it is still needed, and who should take responsibility for it. When asked about leadership, they provide insight into some of the forces that influence the level of leadership development in the community:

> It took twenty-five years as a teacher in Birmingham to make it where I am now. I'm the first female superintendent in my district, and you can believe that I put in my time of hard labor to get here. I make no bones about my mission as a leader in this community; I want the kids under my care to survive to their adulthood. I want safe schools. I want my district to be known as one where young people learn. That's what the board and parents want. I want the teenagers to be healthy, hopefully happy, and if possible successful. But my main goal is to see that they make it through their adolescence, and I'll use what funds are available to reach that end. I've seen a lot of programs come and go in my years in the school system. I don't have any unrealistic notions about some "miracle program" setting all kids on the right path. So far I've trusted the churches and community organizations in the area to provide adolescents with the leadership training that they think is needed, and I think that's worked just fine.

Asking community leaders and school administrators about the importance of developing adolescent leadership skills reveals their perception of the process. Adults typically focus more on transactional leadership skills; they want adolescents to know how to do useful things. Their attitude reflects an adult's need for an adolescent to fulfill roles that the adult values and believes are important. The words of a foundation president illustrate this point: "I want teenagers to speak at public meetings, travel with the board president to the state capital, and be the voice of youth. We need them to go talk to the mayor and council members."

Many community leaders and school administrators believe that all adolescents have leadership potential. They may not use the word *leadership*, but it becomes clear in talking with them that they have a sensitivity to adolescents' ability to be more and do more. A high school principal discusses the role he believes students can play in solving school and community problems, which closely resembles the concept of adolescents as transformational leaders: "At lunch a group of students shared their ideas about how to make the school safer. They didn't say anything fancy—I just appreciated their input and frankness. I like to eat lunch at least once a week with students to talk over how the school is operating, and to get their suggestions. I try to sit with different students every week. I want to know what they think, what's important to them, and how we are doing as a school. I trust them. I think their views have a lot of merit."

The quotes in this section are from individuals who hold varying visions of youth leadership development in their communities. Talking with people like this provides insight into the support, expectations, and barriers that exist for leadership development in a community. Their words reveal much about the adaptability of the community's environment and the deeper and less-visible values of the organizations within the community.

Comparing the viewpoints of these community leaders with those of students, parents, and other individuals who work to create leadership opportunities for adolescents (such as members of a leadership team) provides a measure of the leadership development environment. Are people's views consistent? Where do they converge and diverge? Is it possible to identify barriers, concerns, resources, and support in the community from these discussions? Do people (including adolescents) think about leadership in the traditional fashion, as youths performing leadership tasks (student government officers, club presidents, team captains)? Do any of the individuals share a vision of all adolescents as leaders, with the community creating and supporting leadership opportunities that are within reach of all adolescents? Discussing leadership with community members can be enlightening; it is an effective strategy for gaining information and raising awareness.

The second leadership scan strategy to assess the environment of youth leadership development is surveys. Many communities and schools prefer this formal and structured assessment. The survey strategy has the advantage of providing an accurate description of the current level of adolescent leadership activity and adult involvement; it may also be a better measure of community needs and resources. Furthermore, it is a nonthreatening means of including many different individuals and groups in the process of building a leadership environment. Finally, it provides baseline information that can be used to design and evaluate the community's youth leadership opportunities and interests.

Such surveys are typically paper-and-pencil questionnaires distributed to various individuals, groups, and organizations to assess the current level and type of leadership activities and opportunities in the community. Items on the survey can range from questions about the availability of leadership training to requests for detailed description of leadership activities and opportunities.

At the first and most basic level of survey, communities usually try to determine what it is that organizations are doing. Schools, community agencies, youth groups, and work sites are asked about availability of leadership training, duration of programs, number of staff and participants involved, methods of recruitment used, selection criteria, types of skills taught, and how youths are encouraged to use their acquired skills. Information on locations, costs, and contacts is also collected. A sample information sheet distributed by a leadership program is shown in Figure 8.3. Such a survey often yields a directory of youth leadership development in the community. Multiple activities may be taking place at once within an organization. The best example is a school; it has an array of student activities and programs. We recommend seeking as much detail as possible about the programming in large organizations. Detailed

Figure 8.3 Namosha Leadership Program Information Sheet

Program name:
Namosha Leadership
Program

Organization:
San Claire Youth

Address:
17142 Garden Street
San Claire,   63287

Telephone numbers:
(415) 555-2200

Fax number:
(415) 555-2244

Contact person:
Ms. Nina Marteo, director 555-2206
Ms. Gloria Smith, youth coordinator 555-2214

Program location:
Fourth floor of the Southwest Community Center at the corner of Garden
and Broad Streets in Sandos Park, across the street from Anza High School

Participant eligibility:
Middle and high school girls

Program hours:
School-year and summer activities and
programs, with vacation and after-school
programs

Selection criteria:
Girls with low participation
rates in school and community activities

Target skills:
Stage One leadership skills

Costs:
Varies by program and activity; support available from participating school
districts and United Way Agencies

Description:
A program of the San Claire Youth, the Namosha Leadership Program
targets girls with low participation rates in school and community
activities from Sandos Park in San Claire. Each summer a series of
Stage One leadership retreats are held at the Delgado Center. School-year
activities include community service programs and four weekend retreats.
The Namosha Program is linked to other San Claire Youth programs,
including the San Claire Women's Initiative and Mentoring Youth.

information results in clearer understanding of what is really offered by these organizations, and which teenagers are benefiting from the available activities.

A second level of surveying targets adolescents. Kids and teens surveys (Fertman, 1990) are typical examples; they seek information about the community and school directly from the young people in a community. Distributed in schools or mailed directly to homes, this survey asks questions about extracurricular activities, work, chores, sports, volunteer work, church or synagogue involvement, leisure-time activities, and child care responsibilities. It questions important community issues, such as safety, transportation, recreation, and mental health support. In some schools the student council undertakes distribution of this kind of survey, or in schools with newspapers the survey may be printed in an issue of the paper and students are asked to complete the survey and drop it off at a central location. The resulting information is a picture of how and where adolescents spend their time. It gives a voice to the youth in the community and can be used as a springboard to develop leadership opportunities for adolescents.

The third level of surveying is of professional staff of schools and community agencies, church youth group leaders, and volunteer leaders (such as scout leaders); this is called a leadership activities survey. It contains questions about current adolescent leadership development activities, existing resources (for example, materials and grants), professional training and training needs, and collaborating agencies and community organizations. Those surveyed sometimes prefer informal assessments, where they can express their opinions and share insights from their experience. In these cases, we hold a series of focus groups to discuss the issues.

The three levels of surveys complement one another, providing a broad picture of current levels of community commitment to youth leadership development. Principals, teachers, students, parents, and community members find the information gained from these surveys both informative and supportive of efforts to strengthen their community's leadership development environment. Printing clear and concise data, including the different types of adolescent leadership opportunities available, in a local newspaper is an excellent way to make survey results useful for the whole community. Individuals identified through the survey process as being involved with leadership development can be contacted when forming a leadership team. Distributing such surveys at regular intervals and then analyzing subsequent data allows comparison over a time period, providing a more accurate assessment of the developmental process. In this way a leadership team can track changes in specific indicators, such as the number of agencies, staff members, community leaders, and adolescents involved, and the types of leadership activities available.

Whether a community uses one or both environment scan strategies to assess youth leadership development, doing so gives energy to a leadership development environment. The range and type of available programming and resources varies with the community. The Appendix describes leadership programs that target adolescents in a number of categories that one might expect to find operating in a community. The simple act of disseminating the program and other information gained from the scan is often a first step for a community to expand and strengthen its youth leadership development efforts. Interest and collaboration often increase once adolescents and adults in the community know what is available. The scan process provides a basis for planning future programming to strengthen an environment. After a scan, we usually see an increased effort to balance program content to reflect transformational and transactional leadership, highlight leadership opportunities for youth in the community, and increase adult sensitivity to adolescent leadership.

Challenging the Leadership Development Environment

We now have a fair amount of information about ourselves, our organization, and our community. Next, we want to use this information. It provides a context within which to understand how youths develop their leadership potential and abilities in our orga-nizations and communities. The information forms a backdrop for what is discussed in Chapters Four, Five, and Six; as we work directly with young people, expanding existing leadership services and programs and building new ones, the information collected serves as a foundation to guide our work.

There is a dilemma here, however. The concept of enhancing youth leadership programming in the school, community, work-place, and family seems to be universally accepted and supported by community members. But although people are interested in the information, it is not always used. It makes sense that everyone would see such programming as desirable. However, we have learned to appreciate the fit between the existing leadership devel-opment environment and the effort to enhance and expand youth leadership development efforts: the match between what *could* be achieved and what is actually achieved. Most communities have traditional approaches to adolescent leadership development. They have after-school clubs, school organizations, and community groups and activities. Some personnel at the school, community agencies, and workplaces might even identify leadership develop-ment as something needed by a wider range of adolescents. In gen-eral, though, organizations in the community as they are presently structured and operated really don't permit much innovative pro-gramming.

Resistance

Before we proceed, let's look at a number of reasons for this resis-tance (Baldridge, Curtis, Ecker, and Riley, 1978; Dejoy and Wilson, 1995). We also wish to make some suggestions as to what can be done to lower the resistance and improve the fit in proceeding to develop youth leadership.

There is a lack of support. Relatively few staff members at schools, community-based organizations, and businesses see a need for change, and even fewer are committed to bringing about such change. At schools and community-based organizations, personnel expect to do the same thing tomorrow that they do today. New programs come and go, but there is little pressure to make large-scale changes. The conviction of school administrators and program directors that there is lack of interest on the part of adults in the system is often the kiss of death to any new effort. During one planning meeting for a new program, its administrator talked about how frightened he was to even bring up the idea of a new program in a staff meeting for fear of the negative reaction of the staff. He was defeated before he even tried. As it turned out, he did find that several staff members were interested in trying out the idea. Lack of support is a very realistic concern.

Participation in school and community affairs is peripheral. Schools and community groups tend to be interested in specific issues that affect day-to-day functioning rather than broad issues that affect the community and its members as a whole. The result is that individuals tend to focus on narrow concerns of immediate interest and maintain an interest in these issues until they are resolved (or, most often, buried). Most aren't willing to think about broader, deeper, and more important issues. Leadership development is one of these broad issues, so it requires the inclusion of many settings; implementation of programming in this area is often complex and difficult.

There are differing interests between groups. Community organizations, schools, businesses, and families are all interested in children and adolescents. Their *specific* interests, however, vary from one institution and one individual to another. These differences manifest themselves in contrasting organizational structures, personnel, and philosophies. Each group has its own way of addressing and resolving issues. For instance, the schedules of community agency staff are unlike those of school personnel. Agency staff often work from 9:00 A.M. to 5:00 P.M., while school personnel tend to start at 7:30 A.M. and end their day at 2:30 P.M. Schools also experience difficulty working with community organizations because of the schools' need to meet the academic standards mandated by their departments of education.

Conflict arises. People often think that conflict is abnormal and should not occur. Conflict is normal; it is a fact of life. When it arises, people try to avoid it by ignoring its existence. If conflict in a group is not dealt with, group efforts are usually unsuccessful. At a parochial school in a Midwestern city conflict arose between two members in one leadership team. The conflict was related to teaching assignments and had nothing to do with the new leadership program. But the result was a near-disaster. The only way this group survived was by recognizing the problem and setting boundaries regarding what is OK and not OK within the group. Fortunately, the two team members eventually worked out their problem.

No one is in charge. Initiatives to support and enhance programming for youth are often spread over a wide range of school and community organizations, with no centralized authority or responsibility. No one person is able to make decisions, allocate resources, set goals, or make plans. Things are typically accomplished by a group of people who each represent different organizations with their own agendas. It can be difficult for everyone to come together at once, and when they do meet it is often hard to agree on a course of action. Highly adaptive environments allow those involved to anticipate difficulties and make the changes necessary for survival. Adaptive environments in the school, community, and family life are risk taking, trusting, and proactive. These environments show a high level of confidence and enthusiasm for achieving organizational success, are receptive to change and innovation, and adapt easily to the demands of their environment. We have learned that an adaptive environment of leadership development typically evolves around a small number of people. These can be community and school leaders who consistently work to promote youth leadership and are role models for others around them. There are different levels of organizational environment, depending on visibility and resistance to change.

Gaining Support

What can you do to gain support to expand and strengthen current youth leadership programs? What can you do to maximize your efforts? Resistance should be expected, and to some degree it is healthy. To use the information you have gained, we suggest three effective strategies that focus on what individuals can do personally and within their own organizations to confront the anticipated resistance to change. The strategies to combat it are simple but can make a noticeable impact, given time. The three strategies are derived from work conducted by Fertman, Buchen, Long, and White (1994) in schools and communities implementing innovative programming.

Develop a youth leadership support system for yourselves and your programs. Youth leadership development is a public activity. Working with youth is a challenge for anyone. Teachers often find that getting involved with leadership development moves them out of their classrooms and into the community, where the potential for problems may increase. For the staff of community-based organizations, such involvement can mean that their work is scrutinized as they work in the community and schools. For employers, it often results in additional requests to help with a range of activities and programs.

What is often beneficial for individuals who advocate and champion youth leadership development is to form a personal youth leadership development support system. The aim of such a system is to provide guidance, resources, and support for individuals as they work to expand and strengthen the leadership development environment. Often, a leadership advisory group or team forms over time. These are frequently informal groups of individuals, loosely connected through their work and interest in youth, that can be relied on for feedback and support. At some point, you may decide to formalize such a group into a leadership team, as mentioned earlier in this chapter and discussed in more detail later.

Expanding beyond a small group of stakeholders is the next step in building support for yourself and youth leadership development. Look for people in both your own organization and elsewhere who might be interested in youth leadership development. People within one's organization can provide day-to-day support and offer insights about the organization's unique resources. This support inside your organization is critical because each organization has its own ability to adapt to and integrate leadership development. Some organizations are able to easily modify and expand to include leadership development. Others make small and laborious changes, encountering much difficulty in incorporating it into their system. Developing a personal support system provides individuals with additional resources to confront personal and organizational challenges and obstacles.

Make youth leadership part of "craft discussions." Talk about transformational and transactional leadership as a craft. Craft discussions are small, casual discussions held over lunch, in the staff lounge, or when preparing for board and staff meetings. In order to expand and strengthen a leadership development environment, people need to be informed about and involved with that environment. Youth leadership must be a topic of discussion at every opportunity within the community, workplace, and school. These opportunities include in-service programs, staff education sessions, meetings with administrators, strategic planning meetings, board retreats, program reviews, and budget meetings. Such discussions help focus on the role that youth leadership development plays within the community, workplace, and school. It provides support for adults and youths who work to influence the leadership development environment. It can also be a quick means of disseminating information and getting feedback about new ideas and opportunities.

Be active in the field of youth leadership development. Individuals who work to expand support for youth leadership development have a responsibility to be proactive, staying abreast of changes and innovations in the field. Working to expand the leadership development environment to include both doing leadership tasks and being leaders requires individuals to understand these concepts and be comfortable talking about them. Furthermore, youth leadership development can change the role of schools, community-based organizations, and businesses. It can help alter the ideas held by the people within these institutions about how adolescents should behave. For many professionals, being active in the field of youth leadership development has meant working to increase their knowledge and expertise in youth development, leadership development, and community and school collaboration. Such involvement also requires adults to explore their own leadership beliefs and skills, focusing specifically on their abilities as transactional and transformational leaders.

Leading Organizational Change

We are now ready to discuss how we can work with schools, community organizations, governments, and businesses to change perceptions about how we develop leaders. As we enter this arena, we need to be aware of five hazards that obstruct even the most well-thought-out and sincere efforts (Allen, Allen, Kraft, and Certner, 1987). Be aware of them as you proceed. Following are some ways to avoid them:

Do not fragment efforts. It is easy to make a lot *happen* in a community; the trick is to *sustain* and *support* programming. Often, when we begin our efforts to expand current leadership programming in a community, we attempt too much. Remember that it is better to start small, with a limited focus, and then build on successful programs, activities, and opportunities.

Try not to rely on a limited number of individuals to be the sole leadership champions and advocates. Individual efforts can only last as long as the person has time, energy, and resources to maintain her work. We recommend building support through a leadership team and personal social support network.

Avoid emphasizing activities more than results. People often celebrate what adolescents do: the number of activities they complete, the number of participants involved, and their length of participation. These are important factors, but they are really secondary to whether the teenagers involved are developing their leadership abilities. If nothing happens during a program, then adolescents aren't going to want to participate.

Be careful not to focus on areas other than leadership during leadership programs and activities. Leadership is a positive concept. But its name is often used to attract participants to certain activities, when in fact the program or activity has nothing to do with leadership. Be honest about the real purpose of your efforts.

Do not force adolescents to do it our way. Leadership is not something that we adults "do to teenagers." Rather, the attitude we strive for is that "together we can do it for ourselves." We should avoid entering a struggle between the fact that we, as adults, want the adolescent to learn as much as possible, while the adolescent's tendency is to learn just enough to get by. Leadership is not just another skill for a young person to use to get a job or become class president. It is about changing and refining how adolescents make choices in their lives. This focus moves teenagers to a higher level of consciousness about their leadership potential.

Let us now look at organizations to gain an appreciation of their complexity and their tendency to resist change. It can be difficult for these institutions to attempt new initiatives or modify existing programs and activities to incorporate innovations. For example, it is truly a challenge for schools and community organizations to integrate concepts of transactional and transformational leadership into programs and activities that reach a broad range of adolescents. The risks are perceived as high, and the benefits uncertain. There are also different levels of change, which adults and adolescents involved with schools and community programming have directly experienced (Dejoy and Wilson, 1995, pp. 36–37, based on Nadler and Tushman, 1990, pp. 100–119). Some illustrations of our experience are helpful.

When we first got involved with Coron High School, the school that Bob attends (Chapter Four), the school year was approximately half over. The students were getting ready for midterms. Teachers were concerned with closing grades for the term, grading midterms, and preparing for the second half of the school year. During the first half of the year, a small group of administrators, counselors, and teachers were working on ways to improve relations between the faculty and students. They generated a list of programs and changes they thought might improve such relations. One of the first ideas was to institute a freshman orientation during the summer. It was to be a mix of low-key academic, recreational, and social activities geared to provide information and support for incoming students. Depending on student needs and current issues, the content of the orientation could change. Teenagers usually think these are fun affairs and want to attend; the orientation is part of their high school experience. People liked the idea. (In fact, it was this proposal that eventually inspired the school to think seriously about leadership development.) The school wanted juniors and seniors to lead the orientation. Implementing the orientation was relatively easy. It was agreed that the orientation was to encourage student behavior that the teachers wanted adolescents to adopt. When the level of change is this visible, there tends to be less resistance to it.

However, the deeper or less visible a level of change is, the more resistance there is to the change. Less-visible levels of environment involve shared values that bind people together on a very basic level. At this less-visible level, changes in who the students are have very little effect on these variables over time. For example, at another school where we worked, the student council officers were selected by the principal. The school administration claimed that this procedure historically ensured the highest quality of officers, a good working relationship between school personnel and student council members, and overall stability within the school. Any discussion of modifying the process was strongly resisted.

The scope of the change is equally important. Are we talking about changing a classroom, a whole grade level, a term of work, or the underlying values of the school philosophy? Much of our early work in leadership involved trying to fine-tune existing programs. Working with student council members to upgrade their skills, we typically provided suggestions and motivation that helped teachers and sponsors refine their programs. Eventually our work broadened, and we found ourselves reorienting and redirecting people. When we work with adolescents who have low participation rates in schools and community activities, who are not identified as leaders by teachers or parents, who do not identify themselves as leaders, and who are not experiencing academic or behavioral problems, we provide an orientation session or group meeting for the adolescents themselves, their teachers, and their parents. In such a meeting, the adolescents, teachers, and parents learn about our leadership programs and find out about the activities and opportunities offered. These sessions are designed to help teenagers take owner-ship of the program and underscore the high value that the organi-zation places on leadership within the environment. We target a limited number of individuals.

Some changes, though, do touch the core values of the school or community organization. In the case we've just mentioned of the high school where the principal selected the student council offi-cers, discussion of modifying that longstanding nomination process touched a nerve. It was not only risky but involved alteration of the administration's definition of leadership.

During the past fifteen years, schools and communities have experienced extensive changes that could be classified as *re-creation changes* (Nadler and Tushman, 1990, p. 102). Efforts to reduce vio-lence, support and sustain families, and increase academic achieve-ment are examples of changes that permeate organizations, redefining how they work and relate to each other and the individ-uals they serve.

We have learned that we need to temper our actions in devel-oping leadership to fit the school or community with which we are working. We need to be sensitive and not oversell leadership development to adolescents, parents, community leaders, and school administrators. We do not want to make promises we cannot realistically deliver. We should also be sensitive to the fact that adolescents have experienced many changes throughout their school careers. They have seen initiatives, innovations, and staff members (teachers and principals) come and go; a certain amount of healthy skepticism exists about any innovations or change; adolescents and adults alike are wary about expecting much of new programs and have doubts about how long these initiatives can last. The attitude is often, "We've been there and done that, and we aren't going to do it again." It can be hard to break through this sort of resistance, but not impossible. The first step is to recognize that these sentiments exist and then validate them. Otherwise, our efforts to expand youth leadership quickly lose the energy and momentum they need for new programs to be successfully implemented.

Two organizational strategies critical to expanding and strengthening youth leadership development are (1) inclusion of youth leadership development in the organizational mission statement and (2) distribution of information to the organization's directors and board members. Decision makers in the organization must be made aware of leadership development efforts. Connections of this sort can facilitate better understanding and appreciation of the benefits of youth leadership development. The goal of these strategies is to place youth leadership development within the circle of high-priority organizational values. All organizations have internal priorities, both long-term and short-term, that set the organization's agenda. It is easier to make changes in a leadership development environment if youth leadership is an organizational priority.

Community organizations and schools have mission statements, sometimes called purpose statements because they show the purpose for an institution's existence. The purpose statement of Camp Fire Boys and Girls, a national youth-serving organization with 127 local community-based organization affiliates across the United States, is concise and focused: " . . . to provide, through a program of informal education, opportunities for youth to realize their potential and to function effectively as caring, self-directed individuals responsible to themselves and to others; and, as an organization, to seek to improve those conditions in society which affect youth."

School mission statements are often similar, but they are unique in that they afford the school an opportunity to incorporate into its statement the diverse range of opinions represented in the community. Fox Chapel Area School District in Pittsburgh, Pennsylvania, invited community groups, parents, students, and local government officials to join its school district personnel and board members in writing the district's mission statement. The process included a series of community meetings, public hearings, and focus groups. The result is a statement that represents the community as well as the school and focuses on the role of the district in the community: "Our mission, supported by a commitment to excellence, is to educate citizens who can reach in for ethical behavior, reach up for quality, reach another for service, reach together for the good of the whole, reach each other for mutual respect, and reach out for lifelong learning. Such citizens can change a nation."

Mission statements set a direction toward the goals the organization hopes to achieve. From this statement flows an organization's strategic plan, and thence its programming; if leadership is part of the mission statement, then it is part of the overall organizational plan and programming as well. The steps in Figure 8.4 show what an organization can do to increase its involvement in youth leadership development. They serve to generate organizational support and commitment to leadership development and can be used to revise a mission statement to include youth leadership development. If youth leadership development is part of an organization's mission statement, this is an indicator that adolescent leadership has achieved a level of organizational recognition and commitment.

Another way to expand and strengthen an environment of leadership development is to ensure that organization directors, board members, and school administrators are regularly informed

Figure 8.4 Steps to Include Leadership in a Mission or Purpose Statement and Strategic Plan

1. Establish an administrative structure designed to implement and manage youth leadership development in the organization.

2. Promote awareness of youth leadership programs, activities, and opportunities in the organization and community.

3. Provide staff members with a professional development program to learn about youth leadership development.

4. Introduce the concepts of transformational and transactional leadership models on an ongoing basis.

about leadership development activities. In Chapter Nine we thoroughly discuss sharing information about youth leadership development; however, we make special note here of sharing such information with directors, board members, and administrators, since they are often the least aware of youth leadership development and know only about the formal leadership activities and opportunities traditionally available to young people. One effective solution to this problem is to distribute a briefing sheet containing information about youth leadership development (Figure 8.5). If administrators and organization directors are made aware of the need to change and strengthen programs, they are more likely to try to put those changes into motion. The final section of the briefing sheet targets school board members. However, in modified form it could just as easily be used for community-based organization administrators and their board members, teachers, employers, clergy, government officials, or parents.

Implementing any and all of these strategies can help expand and strengthen the leadership development environment of a community. It is also critical in this process to be sensitive to the youth leadership development programming that is already in place. Such programs find a natural home in community-based organizations, religious institutions, workplaces, and schools. Leadership activities and opportunities already exist in these environments. However, this does not make it easier to expand or strengthen them.

Figure 8.5 Youth Leadership Development Briefing Sheet

Why Support Youth Leadership Development?

Youth leadership development can be a powerful tool. It engages young people in an exciting journey during which they discover new skills and enhance their ability to use those they already have. The teenage years are a very complicated time in a person's life. Adolescents are trying to define their identities, and there are few places that can provide help in this area. Adults don't know whether to treat such young people as adults or children. The answer is that it probably depends on the situation and the adolescent involved. The benefits to supporting youth leadership are many, not the least of which is that it molds youths into more responsible learners who know how to contribute to a system. Adults and youths become partners in a process that helps to meet both of their needs.

Youth leadership development can build students' sense of self-worth and their ability to make a difference. Leadership development gives students the opportunity to practice critical-thinking skills and to use what they learn in real-world settings. They experience positive relationships as they work with peers and adults, and they gain exposure to career settings, improving job-related skills.

What Is Youth Leadership Development?

Developing youth leadership means recognizing that all adolescents have leadership skills and potential, and that leadership opportunities are within reach for most adolescents.

What Can Youth Leaders Do?

Well-developed youth leaders make a big difference in the community. They expect to be heard and they want to make a contribution. They can influence the attitudes of younger children. Youth leadership development also benefits schools and communities. Young people can meet real needs in their communities, and in a leadership program they can begin a process that will make them active citizens throughout their lives.

What Can the Board of Education Do to
Support Youth Leadership Development?

- Spell out support for youth leadership development in a statement of the district's mission and goals
- Acknowledge and celebrate successful efforts by staff, students, and parents
- Link youth leadership development goals with other district goals, such as dropout prevention, use of new technologies, school-to-work transitions, career education, and partnerships between the school and community
- Provide support for program coordination
- Provide time for planning and organization
- Encourage ongoing evaluation and improvement of programs

Institutions and families often like the idea of expansion and in most cases are already encouraging adolescents to realize their leadership potential in some way. However, they are often unclear about what, if any, additional benefits they gain from making extra effort and are concerned about the additional expense, time, and demands that such effort involves. Schools, communities, and employers also may find it difficult to fit in further leadership programming because of full agendas, differing histories of seeking out and supporting leadership programs, and varied access to youth leadership information, materials, and education. The bottom line is that youth leadership development competes with every other initiative and with the daily routines of families, schools, employers, and community-based organizations.

At least three important things happen when adolescents and adults take the time and devote energy to concentrate on leadership. First, it makes a statement to all concerned that leadership is important enough for us to spend our resources—our time, money, and energy—on it; this shows that it has value and is recognized. Second, it lets many more adolescents see themselves as leaders; it shows them that leadership ability is neither distant nor unattainable. Third, there often emerges a demand for more knowledge and skills in youth leadership development.

Through youth leadership development, adults and adolescents begin to see new potential and want to tap it. Knowing this, organizations should work to upgrade their youth leadership development personnel, anticipating the increase in interest. Do not expect an outpouring of demands for additional programming and information; in most cases, people's interest is low-key. An organization might initially respond with briefing sheets similar to that in Figure 8.5. Next, more substantial information can be provided; for instance, a brief report of a leadership scan can be distributed. Some organizations use a newsletter that covers various aspects of youth leadership: education available, a calendar of events, a list of leadership opportunities, and networking opportunities. Eventually an organization can offer workshops and ongoing support for community programming. Addressing demands for more knowledge and skills fortifies the infrastructure. It helps form a critical mass of interested adults and adolescents and builds administrative and community support. This addresses the less-visible values of an organization and community: those we want to shape and modify in the process of expanding and strengthening a leadership development environment.

Building Support Among Colleagues: Leadership Teams

To challenge the leadership beliefs and traditions in the community, school, workplace, and family, you need to build support for yourself and for the process. Without this support, your efforts to expand youth leadership development programming and opportunities will fail. We have found it effective to take time very early in the process to build support among colleagues.

How do we build support for youth leadership development that includes transformational and transactional leadership? Certainly one answer is to build a leadership team. However, a word of caution is necessary. On one hand, getting people together formally or informally can be a very powerful tool. Leadership teams focus attention on teenagers as leaders, funneling energy and resources into programs. They frequently serve as incubators for ideas that others fully develop. In some communities the leadership team is time-limited, in operation for only six to, say, twenty-four months. In others, the team remains as an advisory committee to a community organization or a school. On the other hand, teams can be burdens. People get together for a few times without a clear purpose or interest. The individuals may have very good intentions but simply lack the time and energy to work on an initiative to expand leadership development programming in a community.

The popularity of school and community teams has increased over the last two decades. In the best of cases, they are viewed as bridges among schools, communities, workplaces, and families; in the worst they are thought to be not worth the extra work involved in maintaining them. In fact, within most communities many such groups are already coming together to address community concerns and needs. They are called a team, a task force, or an action committee; they range from those mandated by state departments of education (with prescribed membership, purposes, meeting schedules, and reporting requirements) to ones that are merely loosely formed groups (such as teams of school supporters that work as support networks for the community, operating with very little structure). These groups are found in religious institutions, community service organizations (Rotary, Lions, chambers of commerce), schools (parent-teacher organizations, band boosters), community agencies (advisory groups, task forces), and governments (citizen task forces, review groups).

Leadership teams provide a means for groups within the community to oversee community and school programs and activities, providing direct access and support to programming that targets less than the total school population. They often allow an initiative to gain access to resources, support, and technical assistance not otherwise readily available to individuals. Teams provide a structure for collaboration among the many stakeholders in youth development. Typical formal leadership teams are composed of community leaders, program directors, school administrators, school and agency staff, adolescents, and parents. Businesses are often represented as well. In many communities, the leadership team is a subcommittee of the school district's parent council or parent-teacher organization; in others, the leadership team is a separate entity or subcommittee of a local school board or community-based organization board of directors.

Why form a leadership team? Is it worth the extra work? The answers to these questions are related to an earlier question: What is the community's commitment to leadership development? Nurturing a community's environment of leadership development by forming a leadership team has a distinct advantage over solo efforts; there is much more support to be had among group members. It is all too easy for one person's commitment and enthusiasm to lag over time, particularly when leadership development efforts are not considered a primary priority by communities and schools. The synergy that results when people work together on a team helps sustain enthusiasm and support for the team's effort, even through difficult times.

If you decide to form a team, work from your existing base of support. Invite three or four colleagues who are interested in adolescent leaders to come together to discuss adolescents and how transformational and transactional leadership models may fit into your situation. These individuals must know the existing environment and be willing to become role models for these values.

The number of individuals and organizations that can be considered for membership on a leadership team is quite high. Many schools and youth-serving community agencies identify themselves as working in leadership development, but there is typically a small group of people in a community who are notably involved in leadership development activities. These are often high school student council advisors, school counselors, activities directors, community agency youth workers, 4-H directors, youth group leaders, and church volunteers. Employers, elected officials, parents, and young people themselves are also interested in and supportive of such programming, though they typically play secondary roles in the process. Many times, those individuals interested in leadership development are already in contact with one another informally, if not formally through joint planning and programming. Their activities and programs frequently refer adolescents to each other for participation, informally train staff members to work in each other's programs and activities, and offer individuals information about each other's programs. Therefore, a leadership team often already exists informally. It consists of people already working together to develop the leadership abilities and skills of adolescents. A leadership team can help a community begin to systematically explore its leadership development environment. These teams provide youth leadership sponsorship, resources, cross-fertilization, and support. To encourage such teams, the system must provide time and resources.

Sometimes the motivation to form the leadership team comes in response to a funding opportunity, say from a business or government agency interested in promoting youth leadership development. In some communities, a crisis sparks interest. In such instances, leadership development is seen as a strategy to prevent problems and promote healthy lifestyles. Sometimes a combination of reasons result in the team's formation. The following example of the Reyes City Youth Leadership Development Team (Figure 8.6) illustrates such a combination of events.

Starting something new requires competition with existing schedules, allocation of resources, and juggling of individual commitments. People and organizations alike are often cautious about getting involved with yet another group or committee. They have seen many initiatives come and go, and they frequently have preconceived ideas about which changes are possible and which are beyond their reach. They need time to assess the risks and benefits of getting involved in a new venture. When people do finally meet to talk to each other, they probably find that their individual agendas and goals for the initiative differ. This should not discourage groups from forming leadership teams but rather arm them with forethought, providing a framework for the challenges a newly forming team faces. Such initiatives are sometimes pursued individually and are then dependent on the time and energy of one person. A one-person initiative lasts only as long as that individual can maintain her commitment. Support from other team members allows a group to create some synergy to propel its development. The team as a unit is generally better able to deal with barriers and obstacles than are individuals working alone to address leadership development.

The course of team development is unpredictable. Often the development is part of a larger community process, with ebbs and flows of interest and energy. Outcomes are varied. For example, the Reyes City Youth Leadership Development Team moved ahead to successfully implement its three-point leadership program. At the same time, a second group was formed to pursue strategies in addition to those identified by the Reyes City team. In

Figure 8.6 Leadership Team Case Study

Reyes City Youth Leadership Development Team

In April 1995 Omar Jones, the executive director of the Reyes Community Foundation, called a meeting of twenty-five individuals who worked in youth leadership development. The foundation had a history of interest in the area of youth leadership development initiatives. The meeting was called to discuss the work of the Mayor's Youth Development Council. During the previous year, the council had devised a community blueprint for violence reduction, with youth leadership as one of the fourteen major priority initiatives. At the Reyes Community Foundation meeting in April 1995, attendees discussed their present involvement in youth leadership development and strategies for further advancement. Several committees were suggested. The purpose of one was to arrive at a definition of leadership that everyone could agree on. A second committee was suggested to conduct a scan of current youth leadership programs, activities, and opportunities. A third met to work on development of effective collaborations, and the fourth surveyed programs and youths regarding barriers that block participation in leadership programming.

The next meeting in June was a day-and-a-half-long retreat. It provided participants with an opportunity to learn more about current leadership programming and to explore strategies to expand adolescent leadership development in Reyes City. The foundation coordinated and funded the retreat. At the retreat, participants developed a statement of widely held community beliefs about youth leadership, recorded the "best practices" used by community organizations to develop adolescent leadership skills, and came up with a plan for developing and supporting youth leadership opportunities. Meetings were then held throughout the summer and fall months to reach a consensus concerning youth leadership. Part of this process involved soliciting adolescent feedback and input. In the spring of 1996, the plan was ready to be put into action. Almost a year after the initial meeting, a three-point strategy was agreed upon and implementation began.

When its three-point leadership program was implemented, the members of the leadership team had dwindled from the original twenty-five attending the retreat to eight people. Of these eight, two were from the foundation; the other six were involved in activities related to the initial implementation of the three-point strategy. With successful implementation of the strategy, the leadership team had accomplished its goals. The team disbanded, and responsibility for the program was transferred to the organizations involved.

some communities leadership teams evolve into formal community organizations to provide long-term support for leadership programming in the community, expanding and developing activities, programs, and opportunities that focus on adolescents doing leadership tasks and being leaders.

Leadership teams advocate and champion leadership efforts and help face the eventual challenge of changing the balance of programs and activities. In the short run, a leadership team faces obstacles such as personnel changes, scheduling difficulties, lack of financial support, and resistance within the community. All of these problems can derail efforts to focus community attention and energy on youth leadership. In the long run, it has to deal with the challenge of strengthening the infrastructure of the community to increase youth leadership activities, programs, and opportunities. Another long-term difficulty is carefully choosing the members of the leadership team and then maintaining that team, since its members carry much of the responsibility for determining how youth leadership evolves in the community.

To be effective, the staff of schools and community-based organizations, parents, adolescents, and community members need to view the leadership team as a source of help and support, rather than as a governing body or group of micromanagers. The team's job is to help expand and strengthen the community's leadership development environment, not to get involved in the day-to-day operation of community organizations, businesses, or schools. The most effective assistance the team can provide is in helping community organizations and schools to (1) identify meaningful leadership development programs and activities and (2) help locate resources for developing youth leadership opportunities.

It is the leadership team's responsibility to support a broad vision for leadership development. Once the vision has been clearly articulated throughout the broader community, the team should work with community organizations and schools to determine appropriate leadership development goals and time lines. The vision, goals, and time line help link the school and community together.

Both initially and throughout the course of the team's development, members seek out natural allies: people already interested in and working with youth. If an organization has a history of youth initiatives (not necessarily even youth leadership), this may be a good place to recruit potential members. Looking for individuals outside of this circle—those not already involved with youth development—helps broaden the base of support for a team and provides access to new resources. What is most important, though, when recruiting members of a leadership team is to pay attention to those individuals' personal qualities, including their ability to relate well with adults and adolescents and their belief that teenagers have leadership ability. Among adults, we seek a mixture of new and experienced professionals who are respected by their peers. Parents and community leaders (in both business and local government) are sought. We encourage teams to include adolescents in the membership as well.

A parallel youth advisory team has been found to be effective. Such a team meets to address issues of interest to them. At times the two teams come together, share agendas, and discuss current and future projects. Some individuals might serve on both teams, or act as liaison between the teams. A dual-team approach can be complicated, but the payoff is that more work is completed. We have found teams of adolescents to be especially productive in activities related to communication, program design and implementation, and student recruitment. The parallel youth team also provides youths with additional support and feedback. We have found it very effective to dedicate time at the youth meetings to talking about specific issues and potential strategies to address them.

Leadership teams reflect the community's leadership development environment. For example, a community with a strong, established environment of leadership development might have a team composed of local business and industry leaders, local government officials, and key individuals from various community organizations, schools, and religious groups. Figure 8.7 is an illustration of a lead-

Figure 8.7 Leadership Team Membership

Membership

- Five adolescent representatives
- Two school representatives
- One school team representative
- One local government representative
- One service club representative (Lions, Rotary, Kiwanis)
- Unlimited agency representation
- Unlimited community representation (senior citizens, community clubs, religious organizations, etc.)

Goal

The leadership team meets both formally and informally throughout the year to coordinate efforts of students, community members (borough, citizen, and business), school staff, and community-based organization staff to support and develop youth leadership programs, activities, and opportunities.

ership team from a community with a well-established leadership development environment. Other individuals who may be of assistance include media personnel, representatives of local colleges, and foundation program officers (who can help in locating funding sources). Members of the leadership team should be aware of what is happening in the community; they should have knowledge of the leadership skills most needed and know how they could be used to address community concerns. The team can link adolescents to opportunities present in the community.

Members of the team work to improve and maintain leadership development activities that address the needs of the adolescents and are within the scope of their abilities. The team might also help to develop broad-based community support and funding. Team members work to ensure that all adolescents are involved in leadership development. In the beginning, a team should be an informal, flexible support network made up of people involved in the leadership development activities. Over time, teams can become more formal and structured.

Leadership Team Considerations

Let us now highlight a number of points for a leadership team to consider as their community's environment expands and strengthens.

Size is an important consideration in establishing a leadership team. A team's size varies with the scope of its responsibility; there is no one correct size. Rather, the optimal size of a leadership team depends on the size of the community, the number of leadership development activities, and the number of groups to be represented. The goal is to have adequate representation from all participating organizations without making the team unwieldy. Teams usually range in size from about five to twenty members. Smaller teams tend to operate more efficiently, but large teams can function well if officers and key chairpersons are incorporated into a core committee, with subcommittees assuming specific roles.

Selecting members for a leadership team is an important undertaking and should not be taken lightly. The choices may determine whether or not the team functions effectively. Team members should be responsible, capable, and committed adults and adolescents. Two things should be kept in mind when considering prospective members: (1) the team is to provide counsel to the personnel of community-based organizations and school staff members and (2) members should share a vision of adolescents as transformational and transactional leaders. Here are some important personal qualifications for members:

- A vision for the role that leadership development can play in the school and community
- Motivation, interest, and willingness to commit to the program
- Strong character and integrity
- Generosity and altruism
- Active involvement in community leadership

- Ability to express personal values and beliefs, while tolerating those of others
- Interest in youth leadership development
- Belief that all adolescents have leadership abilities
- Ability to get along well with others, both adults and adolescents
- Belief that adolescents should have a voice in decision making
- Availability in terms of time and location

Adolescents can be a valuable part of a leadership team. They act as equal members and have the same responsibilities and expectations as adult members. We recommend that at least 25 percent of a team be adolescent members. This promotes and reinforces adolescent involvement in activities and validates that adolescents' ideas are valued by the school and community. It is also consistent with the recommendation made earlier to involve adolescents in decision making as much as possible.

As teams become more formal, they may require *approval and support* from the administration of the community organizations and schools involved. Be aware of organizational policy regarding membership criteria, operating standards, and reporting responsibilities. Even if approval is not required, having school administrators and community organization directors recognize the leadership team can be a good way of bringing leadership development to the attention of these organizations, and eventually to the community itself.

Chapter Nine

Building a Community's Leadership Capacity

In the long run, leadership development in a community is likely to thrive if it is endowed with the dedicated work of adults, adolescents, and organizations. Although in some communities a single teacher, principal, community agency staff member, or clergy member has a significant impact on how a community addresses leadership development, it is rare that one person has enough knowledge, time, experience, or energy to do everything that is required. Solo efforts should be discouraged. We want adolescent leadership development to be a communitywide effort that permeates every organization and family. To support the work of the individuals and organizations leading youth leadership development efforts, we have found it important to focus on facilitation skills, program evaluation, and getting the word out about youth leadership development. Our goal is to build the community's capacity to sustain enthusiasm and support for their efforts, even through difficult times.

Leadership Development Facilitation Skills

When working with adults, we emphasize their role as facilitators of youth leadership development. Adults guide and influence the actions of others, both individuals and groups. As facilitators of leadership development, they work with adolescents to help them understand themselves; communicate more effectively; improve interpersonal skills; make decisions; manage their time; work with groups; and participate in community, school, and family activities.

Leadership development relies heavily on the inner strengths of adults as leaders. They model self-confidence and self-assurance, providing an example for adolescents to follow. Leadership development emphasizes adults' interaction with teenagers. Instead of fulfilling their traditional roles, counselors, employers, youth workers, principals, and teachers serve as facilitators and help adolescents augment their leadership knowledge, attitudes, communication, decision-making, and stress-management skills. As facilitators, adults may also take on the role of counselor, exploring with students their interests and abilities and matching them with available leadership opportunities. Adolescents may need guidance to reflect on, evaluate, and make the most of their experiences. Figure 9.1 gives helpful advice for adults who work with adolescents.

Facilitators must be familiar with adolescents' diverse learning styles. Using a variety of techniques to present information and experiences helps a diverse group of adolescents understand and use

Figure 9.1 Keys for Adults Working with Adolescents

- *Avoid issuing orders.* Adolescents resent being told what to do, but they do appreciate knowing what is expected of them. Consistently establish and enforce all expectations equally.

- *Provide concrete examples for the content areas you are trying to teach.* Abstract ideas may be difficult for adolescents to understand; if such a concept is connected to what the adolescent already knows, however, they are better able to apply that information to their lives.

- *Put adolescents' needs before your own.* If an adult is concerned not with the needs of the adolescents but rather with exerting his own power, being buddies with them, or telling everyone about his own life, the relationship between the adult and an adolescent will be unclear and cause difficulties.

- *Honor the differences among individual adolescents.* Each adolescent is unique; encourage her individuality by helping her take risks and explore areas of interest to her. For example, if an adolescent wants to do more speaking in front of a large group, then she should be encouraged to do so. If she chooses another way to express herself, then that should be encouraged as well. Reticence should not be judged harshly by adults.

the material. Cooperative learning methods are especia¹
when facilitating leadership development for adolesc
extremely important for adult leaders to be knowledgeauic ᵤᵣ ₋₋
sensitive to cultural differences among adolescents; this makes it
easier to put activities and information into a context they can
relate to. If the adult leaders themselves don't have access to such
cultural knowledge, then it is necessary to bring in someone who
does have this information to help teens develop a sense of being
empowered to help others and contribute in positive ways to their
communities.

The essay in Figure 9.2 was written by Megan, a junior at an
urban Catholic high school. Her advice is useful for all adults who
are interested in supporting young people in leadership development.

There are several messages that Megan wants adults to get from
reading her essay. One of the most powerful is "silently helping":
not directly telling adolescents what to do, but rather creating situations where they can try out new things and grow more confident
in their skills. The *way* in which adolescents receive information
about leadership is critical in determining whether or not the message is heard. It is important to remember this when designing leadership development efforts. The manner in which information is
delivered can be more important than the information itself.

As youth leadership initiatives develop in a system (a school,
agency, workplace, or religious organization), adults are facilitators of adolescent leadership. Many adults work side by side with
adolescents in leadership activities. This can be a rewarding experience for both; it allows youths to interact with adults on an
equal level, relating to them as colleagues working together
toward a common goal. Adults benefit by being able to interact
with adolescents less formally and more informatively than usual,
because in this new relationship adolescents often feel more freedom to express their views and ideas. This interaction also allows
the adults to provide a model of prosocial, altruistic behavior for
the students.

Figure 9.2 Megan's Essay

Leadership skills are not something an adolescent sets out to gain. At the beginning of high school, a kid wants to be their own person, wants to grow up and mature. While trying to achieve this, leadership skills involuntarily develop.

Here's where adults can come in and "silently help." *Silent* help is very important. Adolescents do not like to be told exactly what to do, how to do it, or the time limit to do it in, especially when the subject concerns them as a person. As a matter of fact, often when an authority figure tells an adolescent how they should behave, it has the opposite effect.

As an alternative, the silent approach can work very well. Instead of telling a kid how to become a leader, an adult can set up situations in which an adolescent has to make a decision, and this can pay off by strengthening leadership skills. Leaving room for decisions to be made by adolescents is a good way of silently encouraging leadership development.

Towards the end of early adolescence, the process of maturing becomes a big part of a teen's life. Being constantly told, either verbally or nonverbally, that they are "just kids" or "can't handle" something can have a devastating effect on adolescents; this sort of discouragement can influence the mind-set of a teenager. The adolescent eventually starts to believe these statements and stops reaching for maturity. Adults need to realize that adolescents are not just kids—they are the future. They are people with ideas and minds of their own who can accomplish great things if just given the chance. That chance is what adults can provide; the chance to make a responsible decision or the chance for their voice to be heard can spark leadership skills that lie dormant in an adolescent.

Of course, there are those adolescents who may not want to grow, who are not responsible and just have no desire to strengthen their leadership skills. That is their choice, but it doesn't mean they are a lost cause. It is important never to give up on an adolescent who feels this way at first, because eventually they could change their minds and become interested in leadership development.

The Role of Peer Facilitators

Peers have a powerful influence on a teenager's leadership development. It is among friends that teens practice what they learn and see. In the case of leadership development, older adolescents provide a frame of reference for their younger peers. They model appropriate behavior for young adolescents and children and help set values, norms, and priorities for the younger ones. Among their peers, adolescents gain social support and offer their own in return. For these reasons, it is beneficial to engage adolescents to

Figure 9.3 Sample of Tasks Performed by Peer Facilitators

- Initiate conversation at the beginning of the activity.
- Support group expectations, helping to set the desired tone for the activity.
- Highlight the themes and main ideas of activities and leadership information (and make a conscious effort to connect the two).
- Change your role as necessary while the activity progresses. Do not carry the group; allow students to have their leadership experience and give them the opportunity to share with each other. When group expectations are not adhered to, or conversations turn away from the topic at hand, use "I" statements to begin a confrontation that once more points the group or individual in the right direction.
- Help participants through activities, but do not lead them. Give them a chance to work through each activity on their own.
- When there is a violation of group expectations or inappropriate behavior, confer with cofacilitators to mediate or confront participants.

work alongside adults in leadership development initiatives, as when adolescents in Stage Two of leadership development are encouraged to participate in Stage One training sessions as peer facilitators.

Adolescents who are peer facilitators require support to work with their peers. With this in mind, we are clear about their intended role and the expectations we have of them. Figure 9.3 lists specific tasks and behaviors expected of peer facilitators.

Leadership Development and Educational Group Process

Adults and peers who work with adolescents in leadership development often serve as facilitators of an educational group. We work extensively with adults and peers to teach them how to facilitate small groups. The work has two foci. First is a focus on the information discussed in Chapter Seven: stages of a group, group dynamics, group expectations, experiential learning process, and reflection. The second focus is on the group process. We attempt to increase individuals' comfort in educational groups by helping them to assess their own presence, set a contract with the group, evaluate group member interaction, and intervene appropriately.

A group leader's "presence" is his or her level of comfort in a group. Facilitators should be aware of their presence; it must be assessed throughout the training and discussed with other adult and peer facilitators. To assess their presence, facilitators must ask themselves how much they are able to be themselves within the group, whether they were well prepared for the group activity, how they present themselves, and the impact this has on participants.

It is also important for a facilitator to set a contract at the beginning of the group session and before each activity. "Setting a contract" means laying down ground rules and stating expectations; it means ensuring that there is an explicit understanding of the purpose of the meeting and the guidelines to follow. The clearer the contract is, the less the chance of complications during the experience. The contract is reinforced during the group session as needed.

While the group session is in progress, facilitators observe the awareness of and contact between participants. They elicit this information from participants during group discussions. After doing so, the facilitators may add their own observations. In the time allotted for sharing, they gather information on the awareness of the participants by asking what stood out for them, what they learned, and whether anything surprised them. During processing, facilitators assess the contact between group members, determining the quality of the interactions among members of the group, between the group members and the facilitators, and between the group members and their environment.

During educational sessions for adults and peers, we also emphasize ways to intervene appropriately. When a participant makes a comment or behaves in a manner that interferes with the development of a group, a facilitator may need to intervene. A leader must deal with both overt and covert behaviors. The manner in which these behaviors are addressed affects the outcome of the leadership activity and the group's overall development. Facilitators should always discuss their observations with other adult and peer facilitators to be sure that their perceptions are accurate. They can then decide collaboratively how best to handle an intervention.

A facilitator must use caution and sensitivity when addressing overt or covert behaviors. A common reaction is to reprimand the behavior. This type of intervention is detrimental to an activity—and ultimately to the group itself—and should be avoided. There are levels of intervention. On the first level, it takes place naturally and is initiated by group participants themselves. If the behavior is overt, participants usually comment quickly. If the behavior is covert, more time may be needed to permit the participants to notice the actions. If the behavior is not addressed by the participants, it is time for the second level of intervention, which involves the facilitator discussing how to handle the behavior and then intervening. These styles of intervention have proven the best, since they protect the cohesion of the group and maintain respect for the rights of each individual participant.

Program Evaluation

At a certain point, evaluation of leadership programming becomes critical to the process of nurturing adolescents' leadership development. In Chapter Seven we discussed reflection as a means for assessing one's own leadership development. Program evaluation differs from self-assessment, however, and becomes increasingly necessary as programs progress. People often have questions about these programs, particularly with rising numbers of adolescents participating in the activities and programs. They want to know what the programs are about, what they do, how much they cost, how much work they require, and whether they really produce the desired results. The answers to these questions help those who are as yet uninvolved decide whether it is worth their time and effort to learn how to implement leadership development programs. For people who already support such programming, the information provided by an evaluation offers support and feedback.

Many of the answers appear self-evident and intuitive. Yes, adolescents are learning about themselves as leaders through these initiatives. Yes, community-based organizations, employers, and schools are involved. Yes, teens, parents, teachers, and community members are excited about leadership development. However, at a certain point in the evolution of a leadership development environment, cheerleading and flag-waving lose their power. Program directors, principals, teachers, community workers, and adolescents need and want more meaningful information and feedback.

We need to offer these people a variety of information, including a description of the goals and desired outcomes of youth leadership development, basic information on the students and leadership activities, assessment of what is being done to build an environment of leadership, and the outcomes and impact of leadership development. In addition, this information serves as the basis for ongoing planning and development of activities. Ultimately, this supports leadership programming and leads to improved practices and student outcomes.

Goals and Desired Outcomes

The first step in answering questions about leadership development in a community or organization is to clearly and concisely specify the goals and desired outcomes of a particular program or activity. To know which aspects of leadership development to concentrate on, one should have a clear statement of what is to be accomplished, for whom, and with what effects. It is important to be honest and realistic in determining desired accomplishments. Figure 9.4 shows information to include in a worksheet identifying goals and desired outcomes in building an environment of adolescent leadership. It is easy enough to include a large number of intended goals in a worksheet, but remember that a program or activity is evaluated as to how well it accomplishes the goals it reports. In addition, although it's a simple matter to revise original goals when the results do not meet original expectations, doing so only hurts

Figure 9.4 Identifying Leadership Development
Goals and Desired Outcomes

Leadership Development Goals
- Ask yourself, "What do we want students to learn?" Specify the desired learning outcome: transformational and transactional information, attitudes, skills.

Leadership Development Activities
- Ask yourself, "What are the leadership development activities?"

Product or Synthesis
- Ask yourself, "What kind of product or synthesis enables students to integrate leadership learnings into action in their schools, communities, workplaces, and families?"

Community Benefits
- Ask yourself, "What are the tangible and measurable benefits that leadership activities offer the community?"

---

in the long run since the evaluation process is designed to provide feedback on ways to improve in the future.

When an activity does not accomplish its original goals, it is easiest to locate the problem if the adults are realistic and specific in the initial step of evaluation. It pays to be honest and realistic in recording the product or synthesis and the community benefits of a program or activity. Think through what the activities involve, and determine what should happen as a result of the activities. Given the intensity, frequency, power, and length of the leadership development activity, what is a reasonable expectation? How does it help the participants change?

How Is Everyone Working to Improve
the Leadership Development Environment?

Once the basic information is recorded, the next step is to maintain ongoing dialogue about everyone's role in building an environment of leadership. This includes feedback from key staff. Typically, staff members report that their lives grow busier as they involve themselves in leadership development, but they also say that they experience increased personal satisfaction and excitement. Although this is positive, it is important to recognize the warning signs when staff become so busy that they feel overburdened. Principals, administrators, and organization directors can also be important sources of feedback, but they too have little spare time. The key to maintaining an ongoing dialogue about leadership development is to be respectful of the scheduling restraints of those involved. A useful way to collect information from these people is to issue an occasional one-or-two-question survey. A focus group that meets once a year is also effective. Include adolescent participants in this process as well. They often provide unique answers and offer insights into the best way to implement leadership development in the school and community. Figure 9.5 lists some evaluation questions that could be useful as part of a survey or as a topic for a focus group.

The goal in this stage of evaluation is to obtain a quick snapshot of what is happening with leadership development, so that those conducting the evaluation can summarize the results and redistribute them to interested individuals. This could be done in the form of a one-page minireport (see Figure 9.6). If adolescent participants are surveyed rather than adults, the results can appear in a school newspaper or newsletter.

Adolescent Outcomes

Part of maintaining an ongoing dialogue about leadership development in a school and community is sharing information about adolescent outcomes. People want to know if leadership development is worth the added time and effort it involves. Does it make a difference in adolescents' lives? Remember that in most cases, people (community members, teachers, agency staff, parents) like the idea of leadership development but may not understand what outcomes to expect. Realistic expectations are critical to the evaluation process, particularly in the early developmental and imple-

Figure 9.5 Sample Survey Questions

For Staff
- Are there leadership development activities and opportunities in your community?
- Do all teenagers have leadership potential?
- State three do's for a successful leadership development activity.
- State three don'ts for a leadership development activity.
- What effects do you see that leadership development has on adolescent participants, especially in the areas of
  - Involvement or engagement in learning?
  - Application of skills and knowledge?
- Can you identify transformational and transactional leadership?
- What change, if any, have you seen in the attitude of community members about young people as a result of leadership development?
- What impact has leadership development had on the philosophy and programs of the organization?
- What impact has this experience had on you?

For Adolescents
- What do you like about leadership development?
- When are you "doing leadership"?
- When are you "being a leader"?
- What skills have you used during the leadership activities?
- How much input have you had in developing and carrying out leadership projects and activities?
- What would you suggest be done to improve the leadership development experience for other adolescents?

mentation phases of a leadership development program. Do teenagers who are involved with leadership development activities learn more, get better grades, have fewer behavior problems, have a greater incidence of graduating from high school, and have greater inclination to continue their education after high school? These are the main questions the school and community want answered. This information can be gleaned from surveys, writing assignments, and teacher observation. As part of the reflection process discussed in Chapter Seven, participants often keep leadership development portfolios. These serve as chronicles of their accomplishments in leadership activities and provide a record of their learning.

Figure 9.6 Leadership Development Minireport

East Palo Alto Youth Leadership Development Initiative Update

A group of ten staff members from local community-based organizations and schools met recently to discuss how leadership development is progressing in East Palo Alto. We asked ourselves: (1) What are the strengths of our program? (2) What problems are we facing? Here's what we found:

What Are the Strengths of the Current Program?

- *Strong leadership team*. The leadership team formed last year has expanded to include five more members. Two are parents and one is the president of the East Palo Alto Chamber of Commerce.
- *Parental involvement*. Parents of East Palo Alto adolescents are involved in leadership development. Several are serving on the leadership team. But more than that, they are gradually becoming more invested in leadership development. Five parents have been involved with community service activities, and two have been lending their time and professional experience to various leadership activities.
- *Acceptance by other teachers*. Leadership development within the East Palo Alto School District appears to be gaining greater acceptance by teachers who have not previously been involved. In the past, leadership development was met with opposition from some teachers, who viewed it as simply an add-on that would give them more work without any real rewards. Now, these teachers are realizing that leadership development is not just an add-on, and that it can be a valuable part of everyday education.

What Problems Do We Face?

- *Transportation*. Getting students to community-based organizations continues to be a problem. There is little money in the budget for transportation. Parents have helped alleviate the strain somewhat, but liability issues make relying on parents difficult.
- *Time constraints*. Teachers need more time to implement leadership development programs effectively. Countless other responsibilities and commitments conflict with leadership activities and projects. Our emphasis on infusing leadership into the curriculum should ease these burdens in time, but for now teachers and students need more release time to make leadership development work.
- *Marketing*. Although the leadership team has begun to expand into advocacy, the community still does not recognize the positive benefits that leadership development offers both the students and the community. The local media focus on negatives in the community and the school district, but they do not take the time to see how positive leadership development can be.

Ongoing Planning and Development

The information gathered about leadership development is best used to support and challenge adolescents to maximize their leadership potential. The staff at community-based organizations and schools typically use the information to adjust leadership activities to tailor training for participant needs and to strengthen activities. They also use it in team meetings to ensure that goals are met and students are engaged in the development process. Sharing such information with students, parents, community members, and administrators and soliciting their input helps strengthen the leadership environment of a community. It ensures that needs identified by the community are being addressed through collaboration between schools and community agencies.

Getting the Word Out

Getting the word out about youth leadership contributes to the community's capacity we discussed early in this chapter. Building enthusiasm and support for leadership within a community demands a consistent and constant pattern of supportive decisions and actions. It follows that a crucial part of this process is clear communication: getting the word out about youth leadership that focuses on transactional and transformational leadership.

The first step in this process is recognizing that leadership development involves the collaboration and cooperation of many different groups of people. Communication among these groups is a vital element in the effective functioning and support of youth leadership development. For example, in a collaboration between a community-based agency and a school to increase the number of leadership opportunities for young people, the participants may include school and agency staff and administrators, adolescents, youth workers, parents, and community officials. Each individual and group will have its own reasons for advocating leadership development. Some will overlap; others will not. Each will have concerns unique to their point of view. These all must be considered and respected when planning and building a leadership environment. These concerns should also be clearly stated to each party. Figure 9.7 identifies common concerns shared by a community agency, parents, and school as they embarked on a collaborative effort to support leadership development. Sharing these concerns set the tone for consistent communication throughout the collaboration, which continued beyond the original intent of the sharing.

Next identify the person or persons with whom you want to communicate and decide what it is you want to say. Teenagers, parents, staff members, employers, and community members are some of the groups with which you will probably want to establish regular communication. Communication can be broadly classified into two categories: external and internal. External communication aims to inform the broader community and groups outside one's own system. Internal communication focuses on building an environment of leadership and initiating and sustaining leadership development in one's own organization. Internal or external, communication does not have to be fancy or extensive; it need only be clear, simple, and timely. Consider how people will benefit from the

Figure 9.7 Collaborative Concerns

Community Agency	Parents	School
Being able to reach school personnel when calling the school	Doesn't interfere with schoolwork	Planning meaningful leadership development activities
Student accountability	Helps child do better in school	Transportation and safety
Managing increased demands for leadership activities at organization	Child likes adult leaders and is well supervised	Student supervision
Students well prepared to participate in activities	Who else among child's peers is participating?	Insurance, liability, and health-hazard concerns

information and how it will help gain support for youth leadership development. Once an audience is targeted, the next step is to communicate the information that will be of greatest interest to that audience.

Principals, community leaders, agency staff, and teachers—that is, those already involved—need feedback. They can use such information to determine ways to strengthen their organization's efforts. Colleagues and community supporters, on the other hand, will use the information to decide whether to become involved. With this audience, the goal is to answer questions and concerns so that they feel comfortable entering into collaborations and offering resources. In this case, the information should be non-threatening, to overcome the anxieties and fears of the audience.

Resource brokers and opinion shapers (for example, school board members, elected government officials, and community leaders) need information that will persuade them to consider changes in policy, resource allocation, and program activity. Community members in general are looking for information on what has already been accomplished. They want to hear about tangible outcomes, particularly those that show the impact of youth leadership activities on the community. Community agencies that are already working in youth leadership want to know about participant outcomes, staff effectiveness, and potential obstacles to implementation. Think about the members of your audience and the information of greatest interest to them, then tailor your information to their needs.

It is equally important to focus on how the information is presented. Packaging and timing of the articles, reports, newsletters, and flyers are critical to increasing the impact of the leadership development initiative. The target audiences—teachers, principals, students, parents, funders, service recipients, and community members—are constantly receiving written information, and competition for their time and energy is keen. Information must be presented in a way that holds their attention long enough for the information to be conveyed.

Information about the positive things young people do is not shared frequently enough. Leadership development can give the community a fresh look at the benefits that young people have to offer. Obvious publicity methods such as newspaper articles and photos and spots on local news programs are certainly helpful, but don't overlook community newsletters, student newspapers, and formal reports to an organization's team and funding sources.

In the process of nurturing their leadership development environment, many communities write and distribute newsletters. A newsletter may include such items as current leadership activities, recent accomplishments, kudos, personal stories, details of upcoming events of interest, and future directions for programming. Topics from a community leadership newsletter are shown in Figure 9.8.

Newsletters often serve as a learning experience for students by providing them with a formal outlet for their writing skills. Another benefit of a newsletter is that it documents for adolescents what they have accomplished. A few strategically sent newsletters can serve as an advertisement aimed at community members who are not involved in leadership development, displaying the accomplishments of students and the positive impact of leadership development on the teens and the community. In addition, flyers and posters are an effective way to advertise particular activities, to the benefit of participants and nonparticipants in the community.

Leadership development activities can also be publicized through the media. Newspaper stories, radio, and television should be used as much as possible. Media coverage conveys a sense of importance to those who are participating in the activities as well as to those in the community who are not: it shows those who are not involved how they are either directly or indirectly benefiting from the activity. The more coverage leadership development is given, the more enthusiasm and interest will be generated in the community. Many community cable companies are required to provide public service access to broadcasting. As part of their leadership activities, students can produce a video that outlines the issue and serves as a communication tool to the broader community.

Figure 9.8 Sample Topics from "Go Ahead" Newsletter

Go Ahead

LEADERSHIP DEVELOPMENT NETWORK PUBLICATION FOR AND ABOUT STUDENT LEADERS

University of Pittsburgh, 5D01, Forbes Quadrangle, Pittsburgh, PA 15260

(412) 648-7196

Volume 4 Number 5, September 1992

To emerge as a leader, one must participate.

To remain acceptable to others as a leader, one must exhibit competence.

What's New at the LDN?

• *Nelba High School* and *Rheedlan High School* joined the Leadership Development Network and offered summer leadership workshops. The City Youth Initiative funded both school programs, and over 120 students participated in the workshops.

• *South High School* is expanding its leadership initiative by offering a series of fall workshops.

• Public Hearings on new city parks and recreation centers are being scheduled for next month. Come share your opinions and thoughts. We need your voice! Call Mike or Carmen at 555–9613.

• *Sullivan High School* is planning a winter retreat for the summer peer facilitators. Call the office for details at 555–8444.

Advisory Board

The 1992–93 LDN Student Advisory Board represents seven schools. Advisory board meetings provide opportunities for students to discuss leadership projects in their schools and expand their leadership skills. This year, board members are designing a leadership training seminar for interested students who did not participate in the summer program. The day-long workshop will be held at the University and will be facilitated by advisory board members.

The following students attended the first meeting:

Regional High School: Richard Smith, Cindy Baker, Greg Palcho

Wooded Green High School: Melanie Chan, David Greenburg, Hal Polenski

North Redland High School: Jamar Brown, Tony Moretti, Rochelle Sanders

Central Chase High School: Allison Owens, Drew Wyrd

Norton High School: Melissa Lloyd, T. J. Greco

St. Peter High School: Ted McNichols, Alice Solomon, Joshua Lee

East Anderson High School: Jane Ellerson, Mia Taylor, Alex Fisher

Advanced Leadership

There are
> *those who*
>> *make things happen,*
> *those who*
>> *watch things happen,*
> *and those who*
>> *wonder what happened.*

ANONYMOUS

Advanced Leadership in your school is one way you can be a part of making things happen. Advanced Leadership is the LDN's way to practice and improve your leadership skills in a unique way. In a group, you have the power to design and implement projects in your school that show leadership. Through these projects, you begin to be seen as a leader and a role model to other students.

LOOK INSIDE and read about all of the projects in which Leadership students everywhere are getting involved, making positive changes in their schools.

What's Inside

Getting the word out about leadership development is the responsibility of everyone involved, but especially the members of the leadership team. If there is a broad representation of involved groups on the team, there will be effective dissemination of information to all participants through their representatives. Representatives also need to share information and opinions from their constituents at regularly scheduled team meetings.

Sharing Information Effectively

Following are a few points to keep in mind when you begin to think about sharing information (Rainbow Research, 1991).

Start with a plan. Think about the information you want to share, and decide which audience and format are most appropriate. You may also want to tailor your presentation to a specific group or individual. Remember to plan ahead; don't wait until the activity, meeting, or program is complete to think about how you will share it.

Keep it simple. There is no need to be elaborate. It is most important that the information shared be clear, simple, and timely. Use brief sections and subsections, and make titles clear and informative. Whenever possible depict information pictorially—in charts, graphs, or figures—and combine these with explanations in the text. Mix didactic and data-rich information with supporting evidence and anecdotal descriptions. This will make the information more interesting, readable, and believable.

Respect adult learning styles. There are three principles of adult learning to keep in mind when communicating about youth leadership development. First, adults are most interested in information that is directly relevant to the projects and problems they're dealing with in their own lives. Second, they're most likely to use information that relates to their own personal experience. Third, different people learn in different ways: some are visually oriented, others prefer narrative text, and some learn best when they hear something instead of reading it. Thus, it may be most beneficial to combine a few different methods of information dissemination.

Packaging Leadership Information to Compete for Attention

In this information-rich society, there is much competition for your audience's attention. Keep in mind that there are a number of ways to disseminate information. Earlier we mentioned a few of the more traditional modes of getting the word out about youth leadership. Following is a list of alternative modes of communicating about youth leadership (Fertman, 1998; Rainbow Research, 1991), some of which may be better suited to a particular audience or circumstance.

- *Executive summary:* This highlights activities and program results. It is appropriate for an audience of principals and administrators.
- *Highlight or brief paper:* An overview of specific activities and programs that emphasizes recommendations and implications.
- *Popular article:* This discusses the results and implications for a specific target group of teachers, parents, or principals. An article may be especially useful in reaching local and state teachers' and principals' associations.
- *Technical report:* A complete report of the leadership development initiative, including background, methods, results, findings, and recommendations. This is a good choice to present to funders.
- *Press conference:* This uses the media for general distribution of information to the community via radio, television, and newspaper.
- *Public meeting:* An information session designed to reach the public. It is good for communicating with parents and can be presented as part of a parents' night.
- *Staff workshop:* This method uses leadership development information as part of an in-service for teachers and agency staff.

- *Clearinghouse submissions:* ERIC educational clearinghouses have an interest in youth leadership. Submit copies of technical reports or highlight papers.

- *Web page:* Many organizations have a home page on the Internet. These can include general information about the organization as well as specific youth leadership information. A Web page has the advantage that it can be updated as often as desired. Other methods listed here (for example, newsletters, brochures, memos) can be used to let your audience know that the home page exists.

- *Memo:* A brief memo concerning youth leadership development can be sent to select individuals and stakeholders.

- *Personal discussion:* This is an individual or small group meeting to discuss youth leadership.

Chapter Ten

Youth Leadership Development in Action

We work with adults (parents, teachers, counselors, youth workers, and so on), adolescents, and organizations (schools, agencies, businesses) to develop, implement, and evaluate both communitywide and more limited initiatives that focus on youth leadership development. These are often built on the foundation of existing programs, funding, interest, and resources. Sometimes new structures are created. Community factors such as local economics, culture, politics, and standards come into play. Working from a scan of the community, we identify gaps and needs in the community for additional resources, activities, and programming.

In this final chapter, we present information we have gained from practical experience in encouraging and sustaining leadership potential in adolescents. First we present examples of young people's work that were produced as a result of their reflection on their leadership development. We have often used these pieces and others to help teens and adults better understand the depth and flexibility of the term *leadership*. They are excellent examples of the adolescent perspective after a leadership experience. The bulk of this chapter is then devoted to detailed accounts of different strategies used to develop adolescent leadership. While pseudonyms were used throughout this book, this chapter is unique in that all the names, as well as the information given, are real. The accounts are meant to give readers an illustration of how leadership development initiatives work in a real-life setting.

My Week at Leadership

We come from many directions,
So near and so far,
To work our group together,
To become our own star.

Strangers to me now are all good friends,
I wish this week would never end.
Only one week, so little time,
To really enjoy our challenging climb.

All my nervous feelings pass,
Time seems to go by too fast,
Now I'm sad, it's the end of the week,
It's hard for me to even speak,
Those sad words . . . Good-bye.

We came from many directions,
Some from near some from far,
We worked our group together,
And became our own star.

—Jennifer Sinicrope

Jennifer wrote this poem at the end of the leadership program when she was entering the tenth grade at Canevin Catholic High School in Pittsburgh, Pennsylvania. Jennifer is currently a student at Penn State University in State College, Pennsylvania.

Though the most visible leaders are those who hold offices in school clubs or activities, there are many more leaders who are not seen as such. People who pursue ideals which they feel strongly about are leaders as well. They lead by example. Although they do not take command of other people, their influence is felt by others and the passion they show for what they believe subsequently leads the ones around them.

—Pete Parkin

Pete wrote this speech when he was being inducted into the National Honor Society at Riverview High School in Oakmont, Pennsylvania. Pete is now living in New York City. He has a degree in electrical engineering and designs Web pages.

The Book of Life

To lead is to work in a group
To work in a group is to cooperate
To cooperate is to understand
To understand is to be caring
To be caring is to be trustworthy

—Frank Somerfield

Frank wrote this poem when entering tenth grade at Elizabeth Forward High School in Elizabeth, Pennsylvania. Frank has since graduated from the Pennsylvania Institute of Culinary Arts and is now working as a chef.

We next focus on three real-life accounts of leadership development initiatives that were designed to expand the definition of leadership for adolescents. The first example is Mt. Lebanon High School in suburban Pittsburgh, Pennsylvania. The goal at Mt. Lebanon was to develop the leadership skills of students in Stage One of leadership development. The second example shares our own efforts with the Leadership Development Network at the University of Pittsburgh to target and support students in Stage Two. Finally, we look at a community and a school in Elizabeth, Pennsylvania, that focused on those adolescents who were in Stage Two but moving forward to pursue mastery in a particular area of interest.

Mt. Lebanon High School: Student Leadership Development Initiative

Schools, communities, employers, and families don't suddenly decide to develop adolescents' leadership potential and abilities;

the process is more subtle. In fact, most youth-oriented organizations and institutions argue that they already develop youth leadership as part of their mission. This was the attitude that Otto Graf confronted in 1989 when he signed on as principal of Mt. Lebanon High School. He found that there was lots of activity in the school, but it was limited to a small group of elected student leaders who were highly regarded by both the school and its surrounding community. The existing program was great for the few students who were involved, but it was a classic example of transactional leadership, and Otto wanted to expand the leadership opportunities to include more students and to broaden the definition of leadership within the school and community. His goal was to develop leadership skills among a diverse range of students who were in Stage One of leadership development.

For Graf, it seemed like a pretty simple process. After all, this would be just another program, and throughout his career he had implemented hundreds of programs, projects, activities, and special initiatives. On the one hand, the process was pretty clear; this was nothing new for him. The steps were concrete, simple, and direct. The first was to prepare the school's staff to facilitate student development. Next was to implement a weeklong leadership workshop for students, and the third was to develop leadership activities for these students. Programming for both students and staff would be designed to give them the information they needed, but beyond that it was meant to encourage them to use their own creativity and individual skills to tailor the program to fit their needs. Graf wanted staff and students to have a personal investment in the program; he wanted them to take ownership of it. He envisioned a sustained leadership development program as a permanent part of life at Mt. Lebanon High School.

On the other hand, the process was quite complex and creative. First, he had to have a clear understanding and vision of a leadership development program that focused on building transformational and transactional leadership skills in all students. Second, he needed a plan that really considered the students. He could only attempt to anticipate the resistance and competition for resources, time, and energy, that he, his staff, and the students might encounter. He wanted to be realistic, without giving up before he started. Third, he had to think about the bigger community. He knew students would need additional activities and leadership opportunities if the program were to be successful. The question was how to develop and sustain those opportunities. Finally, he wanted to be practical about time. He didn't believe the program would be up and running in a single year and knew it might take quite a while, but he didn't want it to drag on too long. He hoped to develop a sustained rhythm for the process.

As the program progressed, three phases emerged.

Phase One: Conceptualizing and Empowering— Two Steps Forward, One Step Back

Graf and a few interested staff members got together to discuss leadership. Eventually, this group came to serve as an informal leadership team with representation from the school and community. The discussions initially focused on their school, teachers, students, parents, and community. They talked about how leadership development could complement their school's existing mission and how they could design a program to fit that mission. They discussed transactional and transformational leadership. A lot of time was spent thinking about adolescents who were not already leaders in formal, informal, or social groups in the school or community. They concentrated on teens who were doing well but were pretty much invisible within their school and community environments. These were kids in the general body of students, the bulk of the school. They talked about whether the environment in the school would support a student leadership program, studied the history of student development initiatives, and raised the question of what would be needed to foster such an endeavor. At Mt. Lebanon, there were certain critical considerations: the interest of the school board, the strength of the parent group, and the staff's willingness and readiness to think differently about youth and leadership.

Even after covering these many topics, it eventually became clear that the discussions were incomplete. As more people grew interested in the idea of leadership development, Graf found that the initiative was being viewed as yet another opportunity to increase the skills of those adolescents who were already active in formal school leadership positions. Parents liked it, students liked it, and teachers who were involved with the students supported it. The problem was that the initiative was going to miss its intended mark.

He had to step back, regroup, and think about what was wrong. People were missing the underlying philosophy of the initiative: the notion that every youth has leadership potential and abilities. Furthermore, the concept of the stages of leadership development was not clearly articulated. Staff, students, and parents still viewed leadership in a very traditional light. They still seemed to think that a person either has leadership ability or doesn't.

For Graf, regrouping meant talking about the stages of leadership development. He helped teachers, parents, and students think about leadership as a personal dimension to be developed and celebrated. He highlighted leadership development in teacher inservices, articles in school and community newspapers, and letters to parents. The hardest part of the process was encountering resistance among adolescents and adults in their thinking about leadership. Being a leader isn't part of most people's lives. It's an abstract concept that isn't seen as relevant—particularly in comparison with doing well on an upcoming test, making a sports team, or getting a job.

Graf also had to think carefully about the inner workings of the school and community organizations. These are public institutions that focus on children and adolescents. They have long histories and traditions. To undertake a new endeavor, one has to begin giving people information as early as possible. When discussions turn to resources, money, students, time, and staffing, people have then had time to mull over relevant information. Therefore, Graf began to talk with parents, students, community members, and school staff about these issues during the first phase of development. As the program evolved, these connections were used as a basis on which to build a network of contacts to support the program.

Phase Two: Planning—Expanding Beyond an Idea

After a few months of discussing youth leadership development in his school and community, Graf felt there was a critical mass of individuals who were interested in and knowledgeable about youth leadership. The leadership team, which until that point had been an informal network of individuals, began to schedule formal meetings and take shape as a cohesive group. It consisted of four teachers from the high school, two staff members from local community organizations, the municipality director, and a consultant from our staff at the University of Pittsburgh's Leadership Development Network.

Once the group came together, Mt. Lebanon was able to proceed to actual program planning. The initial planning efforts focused primarily on forming the program's vision; establishing a time line; thinking about intended outcomes for participants, the school, and the community; formulating evaluation procedures for the initiative; and building support and information networks. Very little was done at first regarding specific programs for the adolescents.

The plan eventually had two parts: adult support and adolescent support. In the process of plan development, the concept of implementing a leadership program changed to creating a culture of leadership development. Leadership would not be something done to the students. Rather, it was to be part of the school and community, to be expected and supported. This change encouraged people to evaluate the environments in their school and community and pinpoint strategies that would promote youth leadership. Student development was certainly part of the plan. However, other types of activities were now considered necessary as well, including different levels of adult education, community outreach, leadership information dissemination, and parental involvement.

As part of the planning process, Graf and the leadership team discussed strategies to target different student populations. It was easy to work with adolescents who were already involved in formal school and community organizations. But the intent of the proposed initiative was to reach a range of students, particularly those only in the first (awareness) stage of leadership development. What made sense for Mt. Lebanon was to conduct a series of weeklong summer workshops to target Stage One adolescents. To support these workshops, the leadership team planned a number of staff education sessions, community outreach initiatives, and leadership activity development exercises.

The final piece of the planning process was to conduct a leadership scan of the community to discover what was already going on in the area. The leadership team looked for potential sources of support and youth leadership activities, materials, and resources. They were particularly interested in what was happening in other schools regarding youth leadership. Once they had this information, the team was able to reassess its decisions about where to focus teacher support, community outreach, and parental involvement. The end result was a plan they believed would maximize the available resources and eventual student outcomes.

Phase Three: Implementation and Evaluation— Focus on Stage One

Mt. Lebanon was a school district with a lot of activities, programs, and resources. It had a strong history of youth development programming. Although the leadership development initiative supported many of the traditional leadership development activities (such as student council, club officers, class representatives), it also sought to build new structures and expand its capacity to develop leadership skills in all students. With this goal in mind, the majority of the initiative's first activities focused on adults; a student program was not implemented until the end of the first year. Instead, a lot of youth leadership publicity and information was distributed to students, teachers, community members, and parents throughout the first year. In the second year, the balance between adult and adolescent programming was more equal, and in year three adolescent programming exceeded adult programming. Student activity has continued to grow since the third year, with the students taking more responsibility for certain aspects of the leadership activities. The leadership development initiative has now been in operation since 1989.

Year One

Three separate adult education sessions were conducted during the first school year, culminating in student summer workshops (Figure 10.1). The first session was held for members of the leadership team and other interested individuals from the school and the community. The session outlined philosophies and models of leadership development; discussed the concepts of group expectations, group development, and experiential learning; and clarified the role of the leadership team. As part of the session, participants talked frankly about their experiences with youth leadership development and their hopes and interests.

Next, the leadership team prepared to implement the summer workshops, learning a step-by-step implementation process. As part of the workshop, members divided up tasks and were encouraged to

Figure 10.1 Year One Program

Adult Support	Adolescent Support
Introduction to youth leadership	Stage One summer workshop
Leadership program design and implementation	
Facilitator skills workshop	

set ground rules for themselves, assign roles, and decide how and when to meet should the group encounter problems. The members learned how to work within the guidelines they set for themselves; they tried to foresee every possible contingency to make the process of implementation as smooth as possible.

Finally, the adults who were to lead the Stage One summer workshops were prepared as facilitators. It was assumed that participants (teachers) already knew how to deliver content, so the emphasis in the workshop was on working with groups. This program made clear distinctions between being a content presenter and being a facilitator. In most situations, adults are asked to play these roles simultaneously, but in this case emphasis was placed on understanding their role as facilitators.

After the adult preparation was complete, youth leadership development activities were initiated, starting with the summer workshops. The workshops targeted Stage One youths. The five-day workshops were conducted by three adult workshop leaders (the group facilitator and two content presenters). Three student helpers with previous experience in the program were part of the workshop staff as well. The student helpers played many roles in the workshop: cofacilitators, workshop support and resource people, and role models for workshop participants.

The workshops were built around a series of structured exercises and activities that helped students assess their leadership knowledge, attitudes, and skills. The subjects included leadership information and attitude, communication (active listening), decision making, and stress management. The workshops were designed to build a high level of trust and honesty (absolutely essential if leadership development is to be achieved) among the students, to facilitate their taking risks and seeking support. As the workshops progressed, so did the students' opportunities to develop skills and seek personal enrichment. In the workshop setting, students prepared personal leadership plans they would work on during their school-year leadership sessions. Everyone was quite pleased with the workshops. Forty students participated, most of them coming into the experience without a clear view of themselves as leaders. By the end of the experience, however, the youths were much more interested in and curious about their leadership potential.

One weak point in the Mt. Lebanon High School program was that despite putting tremendous energy into getting started they neglected to prepare activities that would give the participants opportunities to use their new skills. This made their primary task for the second year clear.

Year Two

In the second year, a local foundation provided Mt. Lebanon with a grant to expand the school's youth leadership initiative. The two-year grant supplied resources to prepare additional adults to facilitate the leadership development activities (Figure 10.2). The team designated a teacher to act as program leader and provided a few periods of release time to use in coordinating the growing number of activities, educational sessions, and workshops. Student leadership workshops, support, and activities all increased as a result of the adult preparation and additional resources. A second series of summer workshops was implemented. However, the school still focused strongly on supporting those students who had completed the Stage One summer workshop during the previous summer.

Stage One leadership sessions, each focusing on a single leadership concept, were conducted during the year for those students who had attended the previous summer's workshop. These sessions

Figure 10.2 Year Two Program

Adult Support	Adolescent Support
Stage One support seminar	Stage One support sessions
Leadership team conferences	Stage One activities
Stage One facilitator skills workshop	Student helper seminar
	Stage One summer workshop

reviewed skills and taught such new skills as building trust within the group, forming a team, planning activities, and gathering adult support for those activities. One result of these sessions was that a range of new youth-oriented activities were initiated in the school and community. A student helper workshop was also conducted during the second year for students who were participants in the previous summer's workshop and selected to be student helpers in the second-year summer workshop. This educational programming focused on role clarification, group skills, conflict resolution, and workshop-support activities.

In the second year of the leadership initiative, the adult preparation progressed beyond preliminary, nuts-and-bolts information; the leadership team turned to acting as a highly functional group; and team members met four times during the year, so that everyone would have a clear view of his role in the group. The purpose of the meetings was to maintain continuity within the group, make sure that members had a clear idea of the program's goals, and simply ensure that the members were communicating with one another. Team members spent time trying to find ways to incorporate more leadership opportunities for young people. They also began to plan for the next group of adolescents who would participate in the coming summer workshops. Throughout the year, as new people joined the team, time at meetings was spent bringing these additional members up to date on every aspect of the initiative and preparing them to help with workshops and activities.

Adult development during the second year was designed to build capacity within the community and school. Members of the leadership team and a number of people from the community participated in the second-year programs, which focused on helping adults incorporate leadership into their regular programming. They showed participants how to fit leadership development into their organization, how to fit workshops into the students' schedules, and how to develop structured activities within which the students could practice and reflect on their leadership skills. In part the program sequence also concentrated on supporting the adults who worked with students. It was an opportunity for the adults to practice their facilitation skills and receive feedback on those skills.

Year Three

In year three (Figure 10.3), the focus on students increased. The leadership team continued to meet throughout the year. Additional programming was provided to team members, adults working with students in Stage Two, and a general community of interested individuals such as parents, school counselors, and community agency staff. The number of students who participated in the Stage One summer workshops increased to sixty. The number and range of activities available during the school year also increased. The school instituted a weekly activity period to accompany and support students' involvement in activities.

We learned from the Mt. Lebanon experience that it is important to be realistic about time, energy, and the process of change. During each of the first three years of the Mt. Lebanon leadership initiative, the number of students and staff members involved in educational sessions increased. Figure 10.4 provides a profile of the number of new students and facilitators who were prepared over time. By the initiative's fourth year of operation, the school had developed thirteen staff members, as well as a number of community agency staff and parents. A critical mass of school staff (teachers, counselors, administrators, and special educators) from various departments now supported the program. In

Figure 10.3 Year Three Program

Adult Support	Adolescent Support
Stage One support seminar	Stage One support sessions
Leadership team conferences	Stage Two support sessions
Stage Two support seminar	Stage One activities
	Student helper seminar
	Stage One summer workshop

four years, 160 students participated in the Stage One summer workshop and remained active in both school and community activities.

The experience at Mt. Lebanon highlighted the need to establish leadership opportunities that would continue the advanced workshops and activities for adolescents. This is essential in maximizing a program's impact on its students' sense of belonging and being involved in their leadership development. Stage Two leadership programming provides new information and shows students how they can use leadership skills in their everyday lives. Stage Two opportunities at Mt. Lebanon included student-led committees, the Principal's Advisory Council, and the Student Leadership Action Program (SLAP). SLAP members met once a month, published a newsletter, and developed and implemented workshops for elementary school students. These activities gave participants an opportunity to use their leadership skills in both their school and their community.

Mt. Lebanon eventually designated a youth leadership coordinator. A program coordinator encourages members of the leadership team to continue their interest in and involvement with the process of leadership development, maintains contact with students, models leadership for everyone associated with the program, maintains communication, and generally provides the "glue" to hold everything together. This person is the bridge between what can be and what is. The school chose an enthusiastic coordinator to link planning and operation.

Figure 10.4 New Student Participants and Staff Facilitators Each Year

	Student Participants	Staff Facilitators
Year One	20	3
Year Two	40	6
Year Three	60	3
Year Four	40	1

Finally, the experience at Mt. Lebanon illustrates two key points. First, expanding how people think about youth leadership is difficult; people come to this type of program with their own ideas, beliefs, and preconceptions already in place. Changing these attitudes and instilling new concepts has to start with the adults and takes much time and effort. We've just explained how Graf approached this challenge and achieved his vision of what leadership development could accomplish in his school.

The second point is that one person can make a difference, but in the long run that person will not be enough. Youth leadership development must be a communitywide effort. Graf provided the initial vision, and sought to institutionalize that vision through teacher and student programming and communitywide collaborations. However, Graf will not be at Mt. Lebanon forever. His stay at the school is contingent on personal interests, community interests, and school politics, which are subject to constant change. The long-term success of the Mt. Lebanon Youth Leadership Initiative depends on the degree to which the people involved internalize the concepts of transformational and transactional leadership.

Leadership Development Network Youth Board

One of the outcomes of our leadership development endeavors with schools and community agencies was an increase in the number of adolescents who sought leadership opportunities. As part of our work with youth leadership development, we emphasize the fact that leadership opportunities are within reach for most adolescents. We encourage schools and community agencies to seek— and if necessary create—opportunities for adolescents to exercise their skills. We see this as particularly important for students in Stage Two of leadership development.

Following our own advice, we formed the University of Pittsburgh Leadership Development Network (LDN) Youth Board in 1992. At that time, more than two hundred adolescents were participating in LDN Stage One development programs each year. An equal number were involved in workshops and support activities for Stages Two and Three at LDN. The Youth Board served a number of purposes. First, it provided a leadership opportunity for Stage Two adolescents. Second, LDN received valuable input, direction, and support from the board members. Third, the board was a useful source of creative youth programming and materials developed by adolescents. Fourth, it served as a model for others to replicate within their own communities and organizations.

This youth board was composed of youth representatives from each of the school districts LDN served throughout western Pennsylvania. The board was a place where adolescents could practice their leadership skills in an environment that supported and valued their efforts. We designed special programming for the young people that encouraged them to work together and take what they learned back to their respective schools. The sessions focused primarily on team building, group leadership, and group dynamics. Throughout the school year, the board met at the University of Pittsburgh to share their schools' progress and to advise us on LDN policies and programs. It was a sounding board for many aspects of LDN. Members aided us in all aspects of the program, including program design and implementation, newsletter contribution and advising, and testing of ideas for innovative leadership programming.

We looked for ways to create opportunities for adolescents. For example, the youths proposed, designed, and implemented an educational program for parents. It was called "Understanding Your Teen." The goal of the three-hour workshop was to share with parents the struggles of adolescents and explore how parents could help support their kids. The workshop was well attended by the parents, who were pleased by the experience. A number of these adult participants reported that they were amazed by their adolescent's ability to speak in front of a group and communicate what really mattered to them. One important benefit of this experience was the increase in respect that it inspired: respect from the parents for the adolescents. It was a successful endeavor.

Other adolescents became involved with conflict resolution. Some were prepared as mediators to work with their peers in the school and community; others worked in elementary schools as tutors. Certain activities developed a focus on writing. Many participants wrote articles for the "Go Ahead" newsletter developed by LDN (recall Figure 9.8). They also contributed to the LDN brochure, helped with the annual report, and assisted in preparation of materials for student workshops. Some of the students made presentations at local conferences and meetings.

The youth board raised a number of issues, one of which was selection and support of the adolescent participants. Our idea was to provide an opportunity for youths who participated in the Stage One workshops and who sought additional support and opportunities to develop their leadership skills. Being on the board required extra effort on the part of the adolescents. It also required a number of outreach activities on our part. Transportation, meeting schedules, and communication were all important issues. We found ourselves working with the families in addition to working with school personnel. This increase in communication with parents was necessary, since the board membership was an activity outside of school. It was in all cases supported by the schools, but because it also extended beyond the normal school day adolescents' families had to fit it into their schedules. This experience was also new for the students we targeted. None of them had served as members of student council or as class representatives; some had never before even been active in school activities. They needed extra help scheduling and planning meetings and activities. As part of each meeting, we took time to review a leadership skill; practice stress management; and review schedules, activities, and commitments. Our priority was that the adolescents become successful in the activities they elected to pursue.

Membership on the board was limited to one year; it was an experience with a beginning and end. Adolescents completed specific tasks and participated in a number of activities. Most members were in their junior year of high school. They participated in the initial board retreat in late September, attended four meetings throughout the year, worked on committees and special projects between meetings, helped with the summer workshops, cofacilitated the board retreat in the fall, and participated in a celebration of their board service late in the fall.

The experience was a model for community organizations and schools. We were not "local" to any of the schools' communities or neighborhoods. We realized that both our structure and our capacity to maintain the board over a period of time were limited. Therefore, we made it a priority to disseminate information to schools and local communities. Each school and community organization that worked with LDN was asked to designate a contact person. These contacts advocated and championed youth leadership in their organizations. Each year we asked the contact people to convene with LDN and the youth board for a feedback and idea-sharing session. As part of the sessions, we encouraged organizations to establish their own youth boards by sharing our structures, procedures, and materials.

Elizabeth Forward High School: Adolescent Community Enrichment

Helping adolescents step up into Stage Three leadership requires us to focus our energy and creativity. Students work very hard trying to direct their lives. We found that at this point in their leadership development adolescents require some experience in grappling with an issue of real concern and interest to them. They don't need more exercises; they need hands-on experience working as part of a group on a real-life issue that affects their community. The Adolescent Community Enrichment (ACE) project was developed to meet this need. It sought to bring the school and community together to provide adolescents with leadership opportunities.

ACE endeavored to give teens more of a voice in their community, involve them in the decisions that affected their lives, and add their valuable input and insight to the decision-making process in their community. ACE represented the belief that young people have much to contribute, that they have knowledge, insight, and experiences worthy of being recognized and capable of making an important difference in the community.

The idea behind ACE was relatively simple (Figure 10.5). It placed junior and senior high school students on the boards of community organizations to serve as active, voting members during the school year (September through April). The project's success depended on three factors. First, there had to be students who were interested in becoming more involved in their community and who wanted to be part of the process of community enrichment. Second, there had to be organizations with individuals who cared about the adolescents' opinions, who believed that teenagers have something important to contribute, and who were willing to work with them to achieve mutual goals. Third, there had to be a commitment to preparation; the organizations and the students

Figure 10.5 Specific Goals for Adolescent Community Enrichment (ACE)

- To find ways for young people to make a difference in their community
- To give adolescents a voice in the decisions that affect their lives
- To provide exposure for adolescents to the processes and the people who lead their community
- To help instill in adolescents confidence in their ability to make a difference
- To provide experience that young people will later be able to use as adults in their community
- To provide experience in establishing goals and in meeting those goals
- To help adolescents learn how to function more comfortably in an adult environment
- To provide opportunities for putting leadership skills into practice
- To help strengthen the relationship between youth and adults and between the school and the community
- To develop and strengthen adolescents' interest in and concern for their community

participated in an extensive orientation process and ongoing small-group support sessions.

ACE was initially discussed by students at Elizabeth Forward High School, its leadership team and leadership coordinator, staff members from the Leadership Development Network, and a number of community leaders. These people decided to recruit a number of adolescents and adults to develop the idea of placing students on the boards of local community agencies. The leadership coordinator took responsibility for overseeing the initial program development activities.

The first step was to recruit students. Recruitment took place near the end of the school year and targeted sophomores and juniors who had participated in Stage One leadership programming. Most were fairly serious about developing their leadership potential. These students worked with the leadership coordinator and leadership team to develop the project. Their assignment was to locate and provide information about community organizations, help make decisions about which organizations were appropriate for the program, and help conduct the participant workshop before the board experience commenced.

The next step was to recruit adults to join the effort. The project targeted adults who were not necessarily affiliated with the school system or school board but who, perhaps because of their concern as parents, had a strong interest in the health and education of the community's youth. The strategy we used was to have members of the leadership team speak to the parents' school advisory council. Announcements to the local school board and the school administration also yielded names of individuals who might be willing to participate in the leadership development program. In the small target community, word soon spread that a new program for students was under way, and simple word of mouth resulted in requests to participate from concerned parents and other adults. A number of parents and community members volunteered to join the effort.

Identifying and Selecting Community Organizations

The adolescents and adults involved in ACE began their endeavors in the summer of 1992, with the hope of initiating the project during the upcoming school year. They held a series of meetings to establish time lines, goals, and strategies for recruiting organizations and students. The adolescent participants had strong opinions and asked many questions about the community organizations. In a number of cases their main concern was the organization's apparent lack of focus on youth issues. We found it very effective to form teams to visit the organizations. As part of this process, we struggled with our definition of what exactly a community organization is. Community organizations have different foci; they concentrate on economic, social, athletic, cultural, or religious issues. The fact is that the term *community organization* refers to different things in different communities, and we therefore need to have considerable flexibility in determining whether or not an institution in a particular locality is a community organization. We should also look at the organization's role in the community. How influential is it in the region, and who are its leaders? Many groups ACE considered had formal boards, while others were informal groups of individuals.

Once we collected information about the types and range of organizations, we determined criteria for working with a particular organization. Certain minimum criteria in identifying appropriate community organizations are considered essential for such a program, no matter what the setting. Suitable organizations

- Have a board designated to advise and/or set policies for some constituency
- Hold regular meetings (at least monthly) for discussion of new and continuing business
- Are a force or influence in the community on some level (service, business, government, education, and so on)

- Demonstrate interest in the youth of the community and willingness to participate in youth-serving programming

ACE began its search for such organizations in meetings with adolescents and adults, where members were asked to list any and all possible community groups they thought would be useful to consider as potential participants. The young people were then assigned to research the suggested organizations: to find names, addresses, and phone numbers for individuals at the organizations and any other information that might be useful in approaching them.

Using the information provided by adolescents and adults, the leadership team members contacted representatives at the organizations (via letter and follow-up phone call) and asked if the organizations would be willing to arrange a meeting to discuss ACE. It was crucial that the individuals representing prospective organizations have a clear understanding of ACE's rationale and goals and know how the program could help students develop their leadership skills and processes, as well as their potential as contributors to the community.

It was also important at this stage for leadership team members to be able to convey their knowledge of the community's unique character and needs, and to suggest ways that ACE could help address those needs. For example, by helping students increase their participation in the decision-making process within local organizations, they could also increase their interest in participating in the community as adults.

Ultimately, the objective in meeting with community organization representatives was to solicit their participation in ACE. The final determination as to participating organizations depended on several factors, among them availability of staff to prepare and monitor the program when it began; additional feedback from adolescents, adults, and other community sources regarding the strengths and weakness of the prospective organizations; and the decisions of the leadership team regarding the suitability of each prospective organization.

Student Selection and Preparation

The initial group of students in ACE were those who had helped to develop the program. In many cases, they had already made links with specific community organizations through their personal research and site visits. Participating on the board seemed like a natural progression for these individuals.

Preparation for the experience involved both the adolescent and adult representatives from each board, so that the ACE experience—new to both—would proceed as smoothly and efficiently as possible. The goal of the educational sessions was to establish a good working relationship between at least one board member and the student who would be working with that board, and also to establish a common body of information regarding boards and board process, the ACE project, and the responsibilities of both the students and the boards themselves.

ACE preparation consisted of a two-day workshop, preferably starting on a Friday afternoon and continuing for most of Saturday. The Friday session with students was designed to prepare them for interaction with the adults and for the leadership role they would play during the workshop, discuss any fears and apprehensions they might have, and remind the students of the skills they learned during their leadership workshop. This initial session was followed by a banquet with the students' parents, where the students talked about their leadership experiences and their interests in and expectations for ACE. This was an opportunity for the students to model their leadership roles with adults, and for the parents to become involved in their children's activities.

The Saturday workshop included both the students and the adults. It was designed to encourage discussion of issues and practical information pertinent to the experience. It was also designed to give the board members an opportunity to see and value the roles the students could play as leaders.

ACE started in the Elizabeth Forward community during the 1992–93 school year. The community organizations' boards of

directors welcomed the adolescents. Six local community organization boards received two students during the first year. The organizations were all small, with perhaps one paid staff person or even
an all-volunteer staff. The organizations included the chamber of
commerce, regional youth activities programs sponsored and
funded by a variety of local religious organizations, a recreational
athletic league, and a community development corporation. One
member of each board was designated as a student liaison/mentor.
The project then started in earnest. The endeavor was threefold:
the adolescents required ongoing support, the board members who
were serving as liaisons/mentors required their own support and
feedback, and many of the community organizations needed help
with their own boards' process and structure.

The youth support dealt with the adolescents' frustrations and
anxieties. It was primarily addressed in a group setting, although
occasionally a participant required some additional individual support. The adolescents' parents were also updated on the progress of
the project. Overall, the young people were amazed that it took so
long for adults to come to consensus. They were unhappy when they
were treated like pieces of furniture and often spoke up about their
displeasure. However, they learned much during the experience:
they found that their community had many issues that they had
never thought about. They also learned that their ideas were often
valued enough by the adults that they resulted in new, more "kid-
friendly" policies. The youths often found themselves conflicted
about what actions to take. Sometimes they got frustrated and simply wanted to quit. At the same time, they had an interest in what
the organization was trying to do, so they wanted to keep at it.
Sometimes they just weren't sure what to do. Most of our work with
the adolescents involved helping them solve problems, locate community resources, and resolve conflicts with fellow board members.

The liaison/mentor support focused on how best to support the
adolescents on the board. The adults needed to understand that the
experience was educational in nature and meant to give youth an
introduction to the community decision-making process, while

providing them with an opportunity to practice their leadership skills. Some boards were highly structured, with defined roles, tasks, time lines, and expected outcomes. The adolescents were given their assignments and expected to complete them. In these situations, the adults had to assess the match between the assigned tasks and responsibilities and the interests and abilities of the students. Some boards were disorganized. The adults in these situations had to help the students understand what was happening in the organization. They connected the students to the organization's process. Where this link was absent, students weren't connected to the organization and the experience was a failure.

We worked with many of the boards to strengthen their process and structure. Having adolescent participation quickly forced the organizations to become more organized. Many board members saw the participation in ACE as a vehicle to obtain more publicity, resources, and funding. It had already provided them with some links to the school district and students who were willing to help the organization. Some organizations were featured in the local newspaper, and students were talking about their experiences in school and in their families. Parents of participants were suddenly calling with questions about meeting times and locations, and other students wanted to know how they could participate. Many of the board members participated in educational sessions on board functioning as part of the orientation. The increased publicity wasn't anticipated by most organizations. They wanted to know how best to respond to the increased interest. In some situations, they had to rewrite bylaws to define who the actual board members were and who could vote. On a number of boards, the teenagers got to vote on issues affecting the organization and community. All of this called attention to the need for us to respond to board requests for technical support. In some situations, we worked directly with the organizations. In others, we referred the boards to consultants and technical support organizations.

ACE continues to function in the Elizabeth Forward School District, placing students on local community organization boards.

The number of students and participating boards varies from year to year. ACE continues to focus on students who want a hands-on experience in a community organization. It strives to provide students with a supportive environment in which they can focus their energy and creativity in a specific area of interest.

Youth Leadership Challenge

The path young people take in developing their leadership potential is unpredictable, with countless moments of frustration, excitement, failure, and success. How they develop depends on who they are and where they find themselves in life. Clearly, adolescents need to be awakened to their leadership potential; otherwise, the danger exists that they will continue to believe cultural stereotypes about who leaders are and how people become leaders. We can help adolescents move past generally held cultural views of leadership to a heightened awareness of their own leadership potential and abilities. The strategies presented in this chapter are just a few examples of what is happening in schools and communities to develop youth leadership. The challenge we face is to support adolescents in finding and following their path as leaders.

Appendix:
Leadership Environment Scan

Upon completion of a leadership environment scan, a community may find that it has a rich leadership development environment, with a diverse range of activities, programs, and opportunities—national, multistate, statewide, multicounty, countywide, communitywide, or confined to a single organization. Often a community finds that it has a commitment to preparing adolescents to be leaders in government, education, business, and the arts. People may be quite pleased to find that a lot more is happening in their region than they realized. However, communities frequently have concerns about the relatively small number of adolescents who are actively engaged in leadership development and about the lack of collaboration and public awareness concerning leadership. Furthermore, discussion of adolescents as leaders and encouragement of youth in leadership opportunities are limited.

The cornerstone of a scan is the list of leadership programs, activities, and opportunities that it yields. Some of the listings are for single educational sessions, while others are multiyear programs that offer a variety of experiences. Most target a specific age category, and some target an even smaller subgroup in that age category, concentrating on adolescents of one race, environment, or gender. The purposes of the programs and activities also vary. A scan may discover adult leadership resources, materials, and programs that are potential resources for youth leadership development. Many programs, activities, and opportunities are found within a community; when viewed as a whole they provide a snapshot of the community's environment of leadership development.

The following sections highlight possible results of a leadership scan; they provide a frame of reference for communities to use in completing their own leadership scans. The sample results illustrate the range of responses that communities receive when they conduct an assessment of their leadership environment. However, the abundance of programs can be misleading. Although these are excellent endeavors, the leadership model we present in this book is a new way of looking at youth leadership development. Therefore it is not to be found in the programs in this list. The programs herein are primarily transactional, rather than both transactional and transformational. We should think of the current leadership programming, activities, and opportunities as a starting point for adolescents to develop their leadership potential.

Schools

Schools are hotbeds of leadership development. Traditional student councils, student-held class offices, honor societies, and athletic teams are the typical sorts of leadership opportunities offered. These opportunities focus on doing leadership tasks (transactional leadership). Extracurricular clubs and activities are another source of leadership development. The level of leadership development available varies from one school to another. All of these school programs and activities are easily identified and documented as part of the scan process.

School Programs and Opportunities Linked to National Organizations

Less clear-cut are those school programs and opportunities that are linked to national organizations. Schools tend to establish ongoing relationships with these programs, sending a certain number of students to participate each year. Many schools conduct some form of fundraising to cover the cost of the program. Nationally linked programs often require the involvement of school personnel beyond their normal school responsibilities. These individuals undertake such responsibilities as information dissemination, student recruitment, and special-event coordination. Programs of this kind tend to focus on students who already demonstrate leadership ability in either formal or informal school and community settings. Some of these programs are listed here:

Congressional Youth Leadership Council (CYLC). Council Office of Admissions, 1511 K St. NW, Suite 842, Washington, DC 20005. Phone (202) 638-0009, fax (202) 638-5218, e-mail <adm@cylc. org>, Web <http://www.cylc.org/>. The council sponsors the National Young Leaders Conference, a six-day or eleven-day leadership forum held in Washington, D.C., for high school students.

FFA. 5632 Mt. Vernon Memorial Hwy., Alexandria, VA 22309-0160. Phone (703) 360-3600, fax (703) 360-5524. A program of the U.S. Department of Education, Future Farmers of America is one of the largest providers of youth leadership development programs. It provides school curricula, activities, and programs focused on youth leadership development.

Hugh O'Brian Youth Foundation. 10880 Wilshire Blvd., Room 1500, Los Angeles, CA 90024. Phone (310) 474-4370. The foundation's purpose is to seek out, recognize, and reward leadership potential in high school sophomores.

Institute for the Academic Advancement of Youth, Center for Talented Youth. Johns Hopkins University, 2701 North Charles St., Baltimore, MD 21218. Phone (410) 516-0191, fax (410) 516-0804. Or: 206 North Jackson, Suite 304, Glendale, CA 91206-4387. Phone (818) 500-9034, fax (818) 500-9058. The center offers courses for academically talented youths at sites throughout the country.

National Association of Secondary School Principals (NASSP). Division of Student Activities, 1904 Association Dr., Reston, VA

20191. Phone (703) 860-0200, fax (703) 476-5432, e-mail <nassp@nassp.org>. NASSP supports student councils and student leadership development programs.

National Youth Leadership Council. 1910 West County Road B, St. Paul, MN 55113. Phone (612) 631-3672, fax (612) 631-2955. The National Youth Leadership Council is a nonprofit organization offering a number of leadership programs and publications.

Presidential Classroom. 119 Oronoco St., Alexandria, VA 22314-2015. Phone (703) 683-5400, fax (703) 548-5728, e-mail <preclass@aol.com>. Presidential Classroom is a weeklong leadership program held in Washington, D.C., for high school students, who participate in seminars, caucus meetings, and "cross-fires" designed to stimulate critical thinking and discussion.

National and Local Youth-Serving Organizations

Leadership activities, programs, and opportunities are abundant in national and local youth-serving organizations. Many national youth-serving organizations support leadership development at the national and local levels.

AFL-CIO Organizing Institute, Youth Programs. 1101 14th St. NW, Suite 320, Washington, DC 20005. Phone (202) 639-6229, fax (202) 639-6210.

American Red Cross. 8111 Gatehouse Rd., Falls Church, VA 22042. Phone (703) 206-6000, Web <http://www.redcross.org/>.

Association of Junior Leagues. 660 First Ave., New York, NY 10016. Phone (212) 683-1515, fax (212) 481-7196.

B'nai B'rith Youth Organization. 1640 Rhode Island Ave. NW, Washington, DC 20036. Phone (202) 857-6600, fax (202) 857-6568.

Boy Scouts. 1325 West Walnut Hill La., Irving, TX 75015-2079. Phone (972) 580-2000, fax (972) 580-2502, Web <http://bsa. scouting.org/>.

Camp Fire Boys and Girls. 3560 Business Dr., Suite 100, Sacramento, CA 95820. Phone (916) 452-4982, fax (916) 452-4989.

4-H Council. 7100 Connecticut Ave., Chevy Chase, MD 20815. Phone (301) 961-2800, fax (301) 961-2894, e-mail <infor@ fourhcouncil.edu>, Web <http://www. fourhcouncil.edu>.

Girl Scouts. 420 Fifth Ave., New York, NY 10018-2798. Phone (212) 852-8000, fax (212) 852-6509, Web <http://www.gsusa. org/>.

NAACP Youth Section. 4805 Mt. Hope Dr., Baltimore, MD 21215. Phone (410) 358-8900, fax (410) 358-3818.

National Federation for Catholic Youth Ministry, Inc. 3700-A Oakview Terr. NE, Washington, DC 20017-2591. Phone (202) 636-3825, fax (202) 526-7544, e-mail <nfcym@capcon.net>, Web <http://www.ymnetwork.net/>.

Outward Bound. National Office, Route 9D, R2, Box 280, Garrison, NY 10524-9757. Phone (914) 424-4000, fax (914) 424-4280, Web <http://www.outwardbound.org>.

Youth Service America (YSA). 1101 15th St. NW, Suite 200, Washington, DC 20005. Phone (202) 296-2992, fax (202) 296-4030, e-mail <info@ysa.org>, Web <http://www.servenet.com>.

Many youth leadership programs are operated locally and regionally by youth-serving community organizations. Such organizations cover issues of education, recreation, religion, health care, and the arts. Following are two examples of leadership programs run by local youth-serving organizations:

Leadership, Education, and Athletics in Partnership (LEAP). 254 College St., Suite 501, New Haven, CT 06510. Phone (203) 773-0770, fax (203) 773-1695. LEAP is a youth service program that provides academic skill building and social mentorship to seven hundred children, ages seven to fourteen, in eight neighborhoods in Hartford, New Haven, and New London. LEAP's mission is to help children from high-poverty urban areas succeed in school and develop leadership among community members.

Youth in Action. San Francisco Conservation Corps, ECO Center, 1050 South Van Ness, San Francisco, CA 94110. Phone (415) 920-7171, fax (415) 920-7180. This program serves students who attend five different San Francisco public middle schools. Participants, called "corpsmembers," attend an eight-week summer session where they learn leadership, academic, and communication skills and are taught strong study and work habits. High school, college, and postgraduate students serve as mentors, supervisors, and tutors for the program. The organization recently launched a new initiative, called Young Urban Leaders, that targets ninth graders.

Civic Responsibility and Leadership Development

A fairly recent development in community leadership development programming for adolescents is the emergence of activities and programs that emphasize civic responsibility. Some of these programs are modeled after adult programs that encourage civic participation and leadership among promising middle managers in the private and public sectors. Many cities have such programs; they are usually highly selective and typically choose adolescents who have already demonstrated leadership ability in formal organizations and activities within their schools or community organizations. The programs are often affiliated with the National Association of Community Leadership (200 South Meridian St., Suite 340, Indianapolis, IN 46225; phone 317/637-7408, fax 317/637-7413). One example of such a program is:

Youth Leadership Forum of Birmingham. 2027 First Ave. North, Suite 405, Birmingham, AL 35203. Phone (205) 252-6559. The Youth Forum of Birmingham is a communitywide leadership program for high school sophomores and juniors designed to expose young leaders to the various elements that interact to form a strong and dynamic metropolitan area. The annual participants are thirty-two to forty exemplary high school students who have demonstrated leadership qualities and concern for their community.

Variations on this model focus on adolescent involvement on the boards of local community organizations. Two examples of these programs are:

Youth on Board. YouthBuild USA, 58 Day St., Somerville, MA 02144. Phone (617) 623-9900, fax (617) 623-4359. Youth on Board is a national program that seeks to place young people on the boards of organizations that address youth issues. The program offers training and consultation in areas such as leadership development, identification of barriers and solutions to youth-adult partnerships, and recruitment and selection of youth board members.

Young Leaders Tomorrow (YLT). Volunteer Canada, One Nicholas St., Suite 302, Ottawa, Ontario, Canada K1N 7B7. Phone (613) 241-4371, fax (613) 241-6725. YLT is a cooperative effort of the Ministry of Citizenship and Culture and the Ontario Association of Volunteer Bureau/Centers to provide young people with volunteer leadership opportunities in their communities.

Youth Service and Leadership

Youth leadership development is prominent in organizations that promote youth involvement in community and volunteer service. The recent trend in linking service activities to classroom learning (service learning) has led to a surge in these programs. This list identifies resources and support for these programs.

Close Up Foundation. 44 Canal Center Plaza, Alexandria, VA 22314. Phone (703) 706-3300, e-mail <cufmail@ix.netcom.com>.

Corporation for National Service. 1201 New York Ave. NW, Washington, DC 20525. Phone (202) 606-5000, fax (202) 565-2794.

National Indian Youth Leadership Project. 814 South Boardsman St., Gallup, NM 87301. Phone (505) 722-9176, fax (595) 722-9794, e-mail <machall@prevline.health.org>.

National Service-Learning Clearinghouse. University of Minnesota, Vocational and Technical Education Bldg., 1954 Buford Ave., R-290, St. Paul, MN 55108. Phone (800) 808-SERVE (808-7378) or (612) 625-6276, fax (612) 625-6277, e-mail <serve@maroon.tc.umn.edu>.

University of Massachusetts, Teacher Education Department. School of Education, Furcolo Hall, Amherst, MA 01003. Phone (413) 545-1339 or (413) 545-4727, fax (413) 545-2879, e-mail <cslric@acad.umass.edu>.

Youth Service California. Haas Center for Public Service, Stanford University, 562 Salvatierra Walk, Stanford, CA 94305-8620. Phone (650) 723-0992, fax (650) 725-7339, Web <http://haas.stanford.edu/>.

Youth Volunteer Corps (YVC). 6310 Lamar Ave., Suite 125, Overland Park, KS 66202-4247. Phone (913) 432-9822, fax (913) 432-3313.

Youth Leadership Support

Community support for youth leadership can be found in many organizations and activities. These organizations frequently focus on adult leadership development training, materials, and support. Information about such activities and resources is revealed through the scan process. The obvious sources of support are businesses, civic organizations, and service clubs. These often devote time to the topic of leadership development. Other possibilities to explore include university and college leadership development initiatives, ROTC programs, community mentoring projects, school-to-work activities, and conflict resolution endeavors.

Association of Leadership Educators (ALE). 203 Scovell Hall, Lexington, KY 40546-0064. Phone (606) 257-7193, fax (606) 257-7565, e-mail <mnall@ca.uky.edu>. ALE is a network of leadership professionals who engage in leadership research, teaching, and outreach programs for promoting leadership development.

Black Student Leadership Network (BSLN). 25 E St. NW, Washington, DC 20001. Phone (202) 628-8787, fax (202) 662-3580. The network includes more than six hundred African American college students, young adults, and community activists nationwide who use community service and advocacy as a means of improving the life chances of children. BSLN trains young adult leaders in community empowerment, neighborhood organizing, advocacy techniques, child development, and effective teaching methods.

Center for Creative Leadership. P.O. Box 26300, Greensboro, NC 27438-6300. Phone (910) 545-2810, fax (910) 282-3284, Web <http://www.ccl.org./>. The Center for Creative Leadership is an international nonprofit educational institution committed to enhancing the understanding and effectiveness of leadership in an increasingly complex and demanding world.

Coro. 811 Wilshire Blvd., Suite 1025, Los Angeles, CA 90017-2624. Phone (213) 623-1234, fax (213) 680-0079. Coro prepares individuals for effective leadership in the public arena. Its programs are designed to bring together diverse residents in a local community. Coro has programs in St. Louis, San Francisco, New York, and Kansas City.

Independent Sector. 1828 L St. NW, Washington, DC 20036. Phone (202) 223-8100, fax (202) 416-0580, e-mail <info@ indepsec.org>, Web <http://www.indepsec.org/>. The Independent Sector's leadership program works to enhance the capacity of the not-for-profit sector to achieve excellence in leadership and management of philanthropic and voluntary organizations.

W. K. Kellogg Foundation's National Leadership Programs. 1 Michigan Ave. East, Battle Creek, MI 49017. Phone (800) 474-1800, fax (616) 964-8007. The foundation supports a range of leadership development programs for youth and adults.

National Conference of Christians and Jews. 71 Fifth Ave., New York, NY 10003. Phone (212) 206-0006, fax (212) 255-6177. This organization fights bias, bigotry, and racism through advocacy, conflict resolution, and education. A variety of leadership programs are offered, including LeadBoston, a ten-month training program for emerging community and corporate leaders.

National Council of La Raza (NCLR). 810 First St. NE, 3rd Floor, Washington, DC 20002. Phone (202) 785-1670, fax (202) 776-1792. NCLR is the largest constituency-based national Hispanic organization, with field offices in Los Angeles, Phoenix, San Antonio, and Chicago. NCLR has leadership development programs, modeled on BSLN, for emerging leaders in the Hispanic community.

Points of Light Foundation/YES (Youth Engaged in Service), Ambassador Program. 1737 H St. NW, Washington, DC 20006. Phone (202) 223-9186. This is a yearlong program for young people who are interested in community service. Since 1991, forty YES Ambassadors have worked in statewide leadership organizations in twenty states and have been trained in youth service, service learning, and youth leadership.

Cooperative Extension System

One important source of programming and support is the U.S. Department of Agriculture Cooperative Extension System, which has programs at each state land grant institution. The Cooperative Extension System offers national, state, and county levels of programming.

4-H is one of the primary areas of programming focusing on adolescent development. In addition, there are four regional rural development centers that link research and extension programs. One of the key programming areas for the four regional rural development centers encompasses both transactional and transformational leadership opportunities. The regional rural development centers are as follows:

Southern Rural Development Center. Bo Beaulieu, Director. Phone (601) 325-3207, fax (601) 325-8915, e-mail <ljb@mces.msstate.edu>, Web <http://www.ces.msstate.edu/~srdc/>.

North Central Regional Center for Rural Development. Cornelia (Neal) Flora, Director. Phone (515) 294-8321, fax (515) 294-3180, e-mail <cflora@iastate.edu>, Web <http://www.ag.iastate.edu/centers/rdev/RuralDev.html>.

Northeast Regional Center for Rural Development. Daryl Heasley, Director. Phone (814) 863-4656, fax (814) 863-0586, e-mail <dheasley@psu.edu>, Web <http://www.cas.psu.edu/docs/casconf/nercrd/nercrd.html>.

Western Rural Development Center. Russell Youmans, Director. Phone (541) 737-3621, fax (541) 737-1579, e-mail <russ.youmans@orst.edu>, Web <http://www.osu.orst.edu/dept/WRDC/>.

References

Allen, R. F., Allen, J. R., Kraft, C., and Certner, B. *The Organizational Uncon-scious: How to Create the Corporate Culture You Want and Need.* Morristown, N.J.: Human Resources Institute, 1987.

American Association of University Women. *Shortchanging Girls, Shortchanging America: A Nationwide Poll to Assess Self-Esteem, Educational Experi-ences, Interest in Math and Science, and Career Aspirations of Girls and Boys Ages 9 to 15.* Report by Greenberg-Lake Analysis Group. Wash-ington, D.C.: American Association of University Women, 1991.

Baldridge, J. V., Curtis, D. V., Ecker, G., and Riley, G. L. *Policy Making and Effec-tive Leadership: A National Study of Academic Management.* San Fran-cisco: Jossey-Bass, 1978.

Basic Behavioral Science Task Force of the National Mental Health Council. *A Report of the National Advisory Council.* 1996

Bass, B. M. *Bass and Stogdill's Handbook of Leadership.* (3rd ed.) New York: Free Press, 1990.

Bennis, W., and Nanus, B. *Leaders: The Strategies for Taking Charge.* New York: HarperCollins, 1985.

Burns, J. M. *Leadership.* New York: HarperCollins, 1978.

Canada, G. *Fist, Stick, Knife, Gun.* Boston, Mass.: Beacon Press, 1995.

Chubb, N. H., and Fertman, C. I. "Adolescents' Perceptions of Belonging in Their Families." *Families in Society,* 1992, 34(24), 387–394.

Cobb, N. J. *Adolescence: Continuity, Change, and Diversity.* Mountain View, Calif.: Mayfield, 1992.

Dejoy, D. M., and Wilson, M. G. *Critical Issues in Worksite Health Promotion.* Needham Heights, Mass.: Allyn & Bacon, 1995.

Downton, J. V. *Rebel Leadership: Commitment and Charisma in the Revolutionary Process.* New York: Free Press, 1973.

Erikson, E. H. *Identity, Youth, and Crisis.* New York: Norton, 1968.

Erikson, E. H. "Youth and the Life Cycle." In R. E. Muuss (ed.), *Adolescent Behavior and Society: A Book of Readings.* (3rd ed.) New York: Random House, 1980.

Fertman, C. I. *Kids Survey: Report of the Community and School Activities Project.* Pittsburgh, Pa.: University of Pittsburgh, 1990.

Fertman, C. I. *Service Learning.* Bloomington, Ind.: Phi Delta Kappa Educational Foundation, 1994.

Fertman, C. I. "Communication and Dissemination: Sharing What We Learned." In J. Smink and M. Duckenfield (eds.), *Making the Case for Service Learning: Action Research and Evaluation, A Guidebook for Teachers.* St. Paul, Minn.: National Youth Leadership Council, 1998.

Fertman, C. I., Buchen, I., Long, J. A., and White, L. J. *Service Learning Reflections.* Pittsburgh, Pa.: University of Pittsburgh, 1994.

Fertman, C. I., and Chubb, N. H. "The Effects of a Psychoeducational Program on Adolescents' Activity Involvement, Self-Esteem, and Locus of Control." *Adolescence,* 1993, *27*(107), 517–526.

Fertman, C. I., and Long, J. A. "All Students Are Leaders." *School Counselor,* 1990, *37*(5), 391–396.

Fertman, C. I., White, G. P., and White, L. J. *Service Learning in the Middle School.* Columbus, Ohio: National Middle School Association, 1996.

Garcia, R. *Teaching in a Pluralistic Society: Concepts, Models and Strategies.* New York: HarperCollins, 1991.

Gardner, J. W. *Leadership Development: Leadership Papers.* Washington, D.C.: Independent Sector, 1987.

Garrod, A. "Psychological Skills of Adolescent Leaders." Unpublished manuscript, Dartmouth College, 1988.

George, P. S., and Alexander, W. M. *The Exemplary Middle School.* (2nd ed.) Orlando: Harcourt Brace, 1993.

Gilligan, C. "Preface." In C. Gilligan, N. P. Lyons, and T. J. Hanmer (eds.), *Making Connections.* Cambridge, Mass.: Harvard University Press, 1990.

Halloran, J., and Benton, D. *Applied Human Relations.* Englewood Cliffs, N.J.: Prentice Hall, 1987.

Havighurst, R. J. *Developmental Tasks and Education.* New York: McKay, 1972.

Hersey, P., and Blanchard, K. H. "Leadership Style: Attitudes and Behaviors." *Training and Development Journal,* 1982, *36*(5), 50–52.

Hobfoll, S. *The Ecology of Stress.* New York: Hemisphere, 1988.

Holander, E. P. "On the Central Role of Leadership Processes." *International Review of Applied Psychology,* 1986, *35,* 39–52.

Ianni, F.A.J. *The Search for Structure: A Report on American Youth Today.* New York: Free Press, 1989.

Juhasz, A. M. "Youth, Identity, and Values: Erikson's Historical Perspective." *Adolescence,* 1982, *18*(67), 443–450.

Kohlberg, L. "The Development of Children's Orientation Toward Moral Order: Sequence in the Development of Moral Thought." *Vita Humana,* 1963, *6,* 11–33.

Kohlberg, L. "The Cognitive-Developmental Approach to Moral Education." *Phi Delta Kappan,* 1975, *56,* 670–677.

Kohlberg, L. *The Philosophy of Moral Development*. New York: HarperCollins, 1981.

Kohlberg, L., and Hersh, R. H. "Moral Development: A Review of the Theory." *Theory into Practice*, 1977, *16*(2), 53–59.

Kuhnert, K. W., and Lewis, P. "Transactional and Transformational Leadership: A Constructive/Developmental Analysis." *Academy of Management Review*, 1987, *12*, 648–657.

Lefcourt, H. "Internal Versus External Control of Reinforcement: A Review." *Psychological Bulletin*, 1966, *65*, 206–220.

Long, J. A., Wald, H. P., and Graf, O. "Student Leadership." *Keystone Leader*, 1996, *29*(1), 21–24.

Lyons, N. P., Saltonstall, J. F., and Hanmer, T. J. "Competencies and Visions." In C. Gilligan, N. P. Lyons, and T. J. Hanmer (eds.), *Making Connections*. Cambridge, Mass.: Harvard University Press, 1990.

Marcia, J. E. "Identity in Adolescence." In J. Adelson (ed.), *The Handbook of Adolescent Psychology*. New York: Wiley, 1980.

Marcia, J. E. "Common Processes Underlying Ego Identity, Cognitive/Moral Development, and Individuation." In D. K. Lapsley and F. C. Power (eds.), *Self, Ego, and Identity: Integrative Approaches*. New York: Springer-Verlag, 1988.

Maslow, A. *Toward a Psychology of Being*. (2nd ed.) New York: Van Nostrand Reinhold, 1968.

Maslow, A. *Motivation and Personality*. (2nd ed.) New York: HarperCollins, 1970.

A Matter of Time: Risk and Opportunity in the Nonschool Hours. Report of the Task Force on Youth Development and Community Programs, Carnegie Corporation of New York, Carnegie Council on Adolescent Development. New York: Carnegie Corporation of New York, 1992.

McKay, M., Davis, M., and Fanning, P. *Messages: The Communications Skills Book*. Oakland, Calif.: New Harbinger, 1983.

Menge, C. P. "Dream and Reality: Constructive Change Partners." *Adolescence*, 1982, *17*(66), 419–442.

Minnesota Women's Fund. *Reflections on Growing Up at Risk: Growing Up Female in Minnesota. A Report on the Health and Well Being of Adolescent Girls in Minnesota*. Minneapolis: Minnesota Women's Fund, 1990.

Muuss, R. E. "Identity in Adolescence." In J. Adelson (ed.), *Handbook of Adolescent Psychology*. New York: Wiley, 1980.

Nadler, D. A., and Tushman, M. L. "Leadership for Organizational Change." In A. M. Mohrman, Jr., S. A. Mohrman, G. E. Ledford, Jr., T. G. Cummings, E. E. Lawler III, and Associates, *Large-Scale Organizational Change*. San Francisco, Jossey-Bass, 1990.

Peters, T., and Austin, N. "A Passion for Excellence." *Fortune*, May 13, 1985, pp. 20–32.

Petersen, A. "Adolescent Development." *Annual Review of Psychology*, 1988, *39*, 583–607.

Raiffa, H. *Decision Analysis: Introductory Lectures on Choices Under Uncertainty.* Reading, Mass.: Addison-Wesley, 1968.

Rainbow Research. *New Genres for Communicating Evaluation Finds.* Minneapolis, Minn.: Rainbow Research, Inc., 1991.

Rotter, J. *Social Learning and Clinical Psychology.* Englewood Cliffs, N.J.: Prentice Hall, 1954.

Simmons, R. G., and Blyth, D. A. *Moving into Adolescence.* Hawthorne, N.Y.: Aldine de Gruyter, 1987.

Smith, H. L., and Krueger, L. M. *A Brief Summary of Literature on Leadership.* School of Education Bulletin. Bloomington: Indiana University, 1933.

Taylor, J. M., Gilligan, C., and Sullivan, A. M. *Between Voice and Silence.* Cambridge, Mass.: Harvard University Press, 1995.

Thornburg, H. "Is Early Adolescence Really a Stage of Development?" *Theory into Practice,* 1983, *22,* 79–84.

Toole, P., and Toole, J. "Reflection as a Tool for Turning Service Experiences into Learning Experiences." In C. Kinsley and K. McPherson (eds.), *Service Learning.* Alexandria, Va.: Association for Supervision and Curriculum Development, 1995.

von Winterfeldt, D., and Edwards, W. *Decision Analysis and Behavioral Research.* New York: Cambridge University Press, 1986.

Wald, H. P., and Pringle, J. L. *A Report on the Evaluation of the Mt. Lebanon Chemical Dependency Prevention Project for 1994.* Pittsburgh, Pa.: St. Francis Medical Center, 1995.

Woolfolk, A. E. *Educational Psychology.* Needham Heights, Mass.: Allyn & Bacon, 1995.

Index

Printed in the United States
47551LVS00001B/26